Google+

FOR

DUMMIES®

PORTABLE EDITION

Google+™

FOR

DUMMIES®

PORTABLE EDITION

by Jesse Stay

WILEY

John Wiley & Sons, Inc.

Google+™ For Dummies®, Portable Edition
Published by
John Wiley & Sons, Inc.
111 River Street
Hoboken, NJ 07030-5774

www.wiley.com

Copyright © 2012 by John Wiley & Sons, Inc., Hoboken, New Jersey

Published by John Wiley & Sons, Inc., Hoboken, New Jersey

Published simultaneously in Canada

For general information on our other products and services, please contact our Customer Care Department within the U.S. at 877-762-2974, outside the U.S. at 317-572-3993, or fax 317-572-4002.

For technical support, please visit www.wiley.com/techsupport.

Wiley also publishes its books in a variety of electronic formats and by print-on-demand. Not all content that is available in standard print versions of this book may appear or be packaged in all book formats. If you have purchased a version of this book that did not include media that is referenced by or accompanies a standard print version, you may request this media by visiting http://book support.wiley.com. For more information about Wiley products, visit us www.wiley.com.

Library of Congress Control Number: 2011940390

ISBN 978-1-118-18129-4 (pbk); ISBN 978-1-118-18132-4 (ebk); ISBN 978-1-118-18131-7 (ebk); ISBN 978-1-118-18130-0 (ebk)

Manufactured in the United States of America

10 9 8 7 6 5 4 3 2 1

WILEY

About the Author

Jesse Stay began his career as a software developer, where in an era of social media he quickly became immersed in the world of marketing technologies. An entrepreneur at heart, he has consulted with industry players both large and small to create some of the most social technologies on the web.

Author of three other books on social media, Jesse has also helped write documentation for blogs such as AllFacebook. com, has contributed to InsideFacebook.com, and has even helped document, as clients, some of the major social networks themselves. Jesse was named by both *Mashable* and *Entrepreneur* magazine as one of 20 developers to follow on Twitter and by *Mashable* as one of 10 entrepreneurs to follow on Twitter. This inside knowledge of the industry has enabled Jesse to understand the ins and outs of how social networks work and set the stage for documenting an emerging network like Google+.

Jesse is currently employed as a social strategist for The Church of Jesus Christ of Latter-day Saints. In his spare time he runs his current entrepreneurial endeavor, SocialToo.com, and is also working on a simple new service for parents to monitor their kids' social network activity called SocialDirt. com. Jesse also consults for businesses large and small as he gets time.

You can follow Jesse on his blog at `http://staynalive. com` and you can always circle him at `http://profiles. google.com/jessestay`.

Dedication

To Rebecca, Elizabeth, Thomas, Joseph, JJ, and Alex.

Author's Acknowledgements

Of course, any of my books would not be complete without thanking my beautiful wife and kids for their patience as I spent two long weeks writing one of the best and fastest-to-production books of my life. And, as always, I am forever grateful to my parents for raising me with computers in the home and always encouraging me to explore my learnings.

Lastly, thanks to my awesome editor-who-wears-multiple-hats, James Russell (go circle him at `https://plus.google.com/103903198087988193655`), who kept me on my toes in a very rapidly evolving social network as we wrote this. Thanks also to my acquisitions editor, Amy Fandrei, who gave me the opportunity to write this book.

Publisher's Acknowledgments

We're proud of this book; please send us your comments at http://dummies.custhelp.com. For other comments, please contact our Customer Care Department within the U.S. at 877-762-2974, outside the U.S. at 317-572-3993, or fax 317-572-4002.

Some of the people who helped bring this book to market include the following:

Acquisitions, Editorial, and Vertical Websites

Project Editor and Technical Editor: James H. Russell

Acquisitions Editor: Amy Fandrei

Copy Editor: Melba Hopper

Editorial Manager: Jodi Jensen

Vertical Websites: Rich Graves

Editorial Assistant: Amanda Graham

Sr. Editorial Assistant: Cherie Case

Cover Photo: © iStock / Kamruzzaman Ratan

Composition Services

Project Coordinator: Kristie Rees

Layout and Graphics: Samantha K. Cherolis

Proofreader: Christine Sabooni

Indexer: BIM Indexing & Proofreading Services

Publishing and Editorial for Technology Dummies

    Richard Swadley, Vice President and Executive Group Publisher

    Andy Cummings, Vice President and Publisher

    Mary Bednarek, Executive Acquisitions Director

    Mary C. Corder, Editorial Director

Publishing for Consumer Dummies

    Kathleen Nebenhaus, Vice President and Executive Publisher

Composition Services

    Debbie Stailey, Director of Composition Services

Table of Contents

Introduction.. *1*

Chapter 1: Leaping into Google+ 5

Creating Your Account... 5
    Getting an invite................................. 6
    Filling out your information 6
Setting Up Your Profile — the Basics...................... 8
Setting Up Your Profile — Advanced 11
    Filling out your About page....................... 11
    Setting your circle settings
        (say that five times fast!) 14
    Setting other privacy options 16
Understanding the +1 18
Following Others on Google+ 19
    Picking whom to follow.......................... 19
    Organizing your followers 20
Using the Sandbar on Other Google Products 21
Making Your First Post.. 22
    Choosing your message......................... 22
    Choosing your destination 23
    Notifying friends who haven't circled you 25

Chapter 2: Boggling Over Circles and Privacy........27

Understanding Circles... 27
Creating Circles.. 29
    Dragging people into the "Drop Here
        to Create a New Circle" circle 29
    Clicking the "Drop Here to Create a
        New Circle" circle 31
    Mousing over people's names to configure circles... 31
Adding People to Your Circles 32
Consuming the Content for Each Circle.......................... 33
Inviting New People to Google+ 36
Setting Who Can See Your Profile.............................. 38

Chapter 3: Posting to Google+ 43

Knowing What to Post 43
    Sharing posts with only close friends and family 44
    Posting to journal your life 46
    Posting to communicate with specific groups 46
    Posting to increase the number of
        people circling you 47
Picking Your Audience 48
    Posting to circles 48
    Posting to individuals 49
    Posting to e-mail addresses 50
    Knowing who will see your posts
        and how they'll see the posts 50
Sharing, Resharing, and Commenting on Posts 51
    Resharing others' posts 51
    Getting people to comment on your posts 53
    Mentioning others in posts and comments 53
Moderating Your Posts 54
    Editing your posts 54
    Deleting your posts 55
    Muting posts 55
    Deleting comments 55
    Disabling comments or reshares 56
Dealing with Trolls 57
    Handling trolls short of blocking them 57
    Ignoring trolls when you just want
        a little peace and quiet 58
    Blocking trolls when you've just had enough 60

Chapter 4: Hanging Out with Friends 63

Starting Your First Hangout 64
    Getting your video "just right" 64
    Picking whom to hangout with 64
Administering Your Hangout 66

Chapter 5: Finding Content with Sparks 69

Picking Your Sparks 69
Reading and Interacting with Sparks 71

Chapter 6: Gaming with Google+ 73

Finding Games to Play 73
Reading the Games Stream 76
Challenging Your Friends 77

Chapter 7: Abiding by Social Network Etiquette 79

Deciding What to Post 80
    Guidelines for posting 81
    Commenting on others' posts 82
Knowing When to Tag Other People 83
E-mailing Others and Knowing When You Should 85
Knowing When to Back Away
    (And How to Avoid Trolling) 86

Chapter 8: Using Google+ on Mobile Devices 89

Understanding the Google+ Mobile App Experience 89
    Using Google+ on an iOS or Android device 90
    Using Google+ features only on Android devices 91
    Using Google+ on the mobile web 95
Posting to Google+ on a Mobile Device 96
    Uploading photos on a mobile device 98
    Checking in 100
Viewing the "Nearby" Stream 101
Using Huddles to Chat with Groups 102

Chapter 9: Using Google+ Photos 105

Viewing Your Photos 105
    Viewing photos taken of you 106
    Viewing photos taken on your phone 107
    Viewing photos you've uploaded 108
Viewing Photos from Your Circles 110
Uploading New Photos 111
Tagging Others in Photos 113
Configuring Privacy Settings for Your Photos 114
Sharing Your Photos 115

Chapter 10: Liberating (Exporting and Backing Up) Your G+ Data 117

Knowing What You Can Back Up 117
Backing Up Your Data 118

**Chapter 11: Ten Third-Party Applications
You Can Use Right Now.......................123**

    Klout 124
    Reader to Plus 124
    Extended Share for Google+ 124
    Google+ Hangout Check 125
    Replies and More for Google+ 125
    Plus Minus.. 125
    Surplus 126
    +Photo Zoom 126
    SocialStatistics.com.. 126
    G+ Stream Pause 127
    Go for More!.. 127

Index... *129*

Introduction

● ●

Chances are you're one of the 750 million or so users of Facebook, or maybe you've tried Twitter or another social network. Google has responded to the lively interest in social networking with one of its own called Google+ (also known as "Google Plus" or even just "g+"), and Google+ is quickly becoming a serious alternative for those looking for a new environment to play in.

At an estimated 30 million or so users in just one month, Google+ is clearly a force to be reckoned with. Google has figured out a way to integrate the network with all of its major products, which becomes evident the minute you sign up for the service!

Why the "plus," you might ask? Rumor has it, Google needed a place to bring all of its apps into one place, making every piece of Google part of a social experience. Now, instead of just a bunch of web apps, Google is becoming one large social network — Google+ ties everything together right at the heart of Google. This spirit of cohesion between all things Google will become even more evident as Google+ grows, I'm quite sure, and my hope is that this book will make the transition easy so that you can enjoy this network as much as I do.

About This Book

You don't have to be new to social media to read this book! The truth is, according to Facebook stats regarding use, you may already log in to Facebook at least once daily, and may even have spent more than a couple of years using the service. This book is for new users of Google+ who are coming from social networks like Facebook and Twitter. Google+ won't be exactly what you're used to, which is why you need this book!

Because Google+ is less than six months old, in writing this book I want to document the service and provide a way for new users coming from other social networks to become accustomed to the parts of Google+ that may not seem familiar.

At the same time, because Google+ is a new service, I fully expect it to change quickly. For that reason I've created this portable edition to cover just enough and yet allow for some flexibility for when the service does change.

Spend some time perusing Google+, and feel free to use this book as you like. My intention is that by reading this book you will get past the "weirdness" of the new network and past any concerns you may have with it. Consider this book your friend as you explore this new social network.

Foolish Assumptions

I don't assume that you know much about social media or the Internet to use this book. Previous experience with Facebook or Twitter or another social network may help, but for the most part I've written this book so that all readers can easily understand and use it.

There are some things I do assume you know, however. For instance, you should have at least some basic knowledge of using a computer. Ideally, for parts like Chapter 4 on hangouts, you should have a working webcam attached to your computer. If you read Chapter 8, you should have a mobile device and know how to use it.

Even if you don't understand computers or webcams or mobile devices, though, at least give this book a try. You may learn a little along the way. Ask your kids if you're older — they probably know how to help you. Find your resident computer geek.

Icons Used in This Book

You'll see little icons scattered throughout the book. These icons flag additional, helpful information.

Tips provide beneficial information and advice that I've picked up using Google+. I share these tidbits with you in case they can enhance your experience, too.

Pay close attention to these icons! This information may help keep you out of trouble!

When I have a piece of information that I want you to keep in the back of your head or bring back to your attention, I use this icon to remind you of that fact. Tie a string around your finger, write it down, or do what you need to not forget these things!

These icons flag technical information that a typical web user may not care about and can skip at will. Not that it isn't interesting, but it's not necessary for getting the basics of Google+ down. Read these to find out about the inner nuts and bolts of the features of Google+.

Where to Go from Here

Although, in general, I suggest beginning with the first chapter and reading the book sequentially, it's organized so that you can pick and choose which pieces of Google+ you want to find out about first. So, please feel free to skip around as you like!

Keep this book with you as you use Google+ for the first time. As you come upon parts that you're not so sure about, refer to this book and let it guide you through the process.

If you have any questions, you can always contact me on Google+ at http://profiles.google.com/jessestay.

Or, if you haven't created a Google+ account yet and still need a way to contact me, you can go to my Facebook Page for this book at `http://facebook.com/googleplusportable`. Don't hesitate to ask questions! I love to meet my readers, and I love to help where I can. Go to both places now, circle me, and like the Facebook Page!

If you still can't get enough of noisy Google+ folks to follow, check out this book's editor's page, too. His name is James Russell and the shortened URL for his Google+ profile is `http://goo.gl/Ci8jb` (the real URL is `https://plus.google.com/103903198087988193655` — obviously totally obnoxious — because Google+ hasn't shortened his profile URL yet).

Occasionally, we have updates to our technology books. If this book does have technical updates, they will be posted here: `www.dummies.com/go/googleplusfordummies portableedition`

Chapter 1

Leaping into Google+

In This Chapter

▶ Figuring out how to use Google+

▶ Getting familiar with the Google+ interface

▶ Registering for Google+

▶ Understanding your Google+ profile

*Y*ou've probably gotten the invitation by now—"so and so has invited you to Google+." Or maybe you've seen your friends on Facebook asking if anyone wants a Google+ invite, and you're curious about this new-fangled social network by Google. Whatever your reasoning, your interest is piqued — now what?

The best way to learn about any social network is to just dive in and use it. Just like driving a car, anyone can tell you how to get in, turn the keys, and step on the gas, but until you get in and start driving and run over a few curbs and bushes, you'll never really learn what driving a car is all about.

The first step to beginning your quest to use Google+ is to, like the car example, just dive in, create an account, and start using it! In this chapter, I show you how to do just that, from creating your account, to finding and organizing contacts, to posting your first post.

Creating Your Account

Creating your Google+ account is easy, you simply need to visit http://plus.google.com and sign up! You'll have to create a Google account if you don't already have one, or you just need to log in with an existing account to access your new Google+ profile. Then you just enter some basic information about yourself to get started.

Signing Up

When Google+ was first released to the public it was invitation-only, but luckily that's no longer the case. As of this writing, Google+ is in open beta and anyone can join. You still may get invited, though; if you do get an invitation in your e-mail you'll just need to click on the link in the e-mail to get started creating your account.

If you want to be invited by e-mail, go ahead and ask for an invite at `http://facebook.com/googleplusportable`! Yes, even though this book is about Google+, it has a Facebook Page so that users like you or your friends who haven't yet joined Google+ can come and find out more about Google+, ask for invites, and get started with the service. Also, because it's so new, Google+ doesn't yet have a way for business profiles to exist on the service, so a Facebook Page is the next-best thing in lieu of a dedicated Google+ page to provide a social media home for this book.

Filling out your information

Now that you have access to the service, it's time to create your account and start filling out some basic information.

If you know you have an invite but can't find the e-mail, just go to `http://plus.google.com`. If you've already received an invite, going to that URL will accomplish the same thing.

Just follow these steps to get going:

1. **Log in to your e-mail account and click the Join Google+ or the Learn More About Google+ link in your invite e-mail.**

   A page that looks like the one in Figure 1-1 appears.

The name of the link in this step depends on whether you were invited specifically or by someone who is a member sharing a post with you on Google+ via e-mail (you'll learn more about how to do this later in the book).

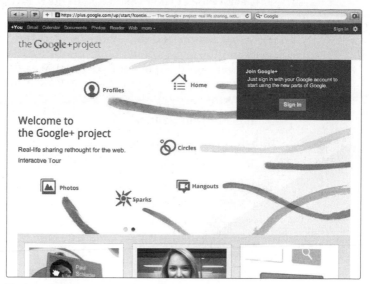

Figure 1-1: Signing in with Google account information.

2. **Click Sign In.**

   You are whisked off to a login form where you enter your Google account credentials.

3. **Sign in with your Google account by entering your Google username and password.**

   Don't have a Google account? You can create one on this page by clicking the "Create an account now" link below the login box. Just follow the steps to create your Google account; then start this list again with Step 1.

   Google now prompts you to fill out some basic information for your Google+ profile.

4. **Enter your name (this will likely be filled in for you).**

Make sure you enter your real name! Google+ is about real people. Even if people recognize you by a pseudonym, your account can get blocked if you don't use your real name here. In many ways, Google is even pickier than Facebook in this regard, but it's to encourage real interactions with people.

Google is rumored to be working on better ways to allow other types of personas on the system, so if this isn't good enough for you, keep watching and an option that works well for you may likely appear in the future.

5. **Indicate your gender.**

6. **Select a profile photo.**

Google+ asks you to size your photo.

7. **Select the area you want for your profile photo and choose Set as Profile Photo.**

8. **When prompted, decide if you want Google to use your information to personalize content and ads on non-Google websites by checking or leaving the box unchecked.**

This enables more personalized ads and content on the Google sites you visit, but it is optional if you feel uncomfortable selecting this option.

9. **Click Join.**

You're done! You can now start using Google+.

Setting Up Your Profile — the Basics

Now that you're in Google+, you'll probably want to configure a little more information about yourself. After initially setting up your profile, Google+ immediately takes you to a site where you can fill out more profile information, as shown in

Figure 1-2. If you're really in a rush, just click Continue to My Profile and you can get started, but it might be to your benefit to enter at least a little bit about yourself to ensure that you get the best recommendations about people to follow — and perhaps more importantly because people with blank profiles generally are ignored by people trying to find great people to *circle* (the *follow* of Google+). If you want to know more about what circles are, skip to Chapter 2 where I cover them in-depth.

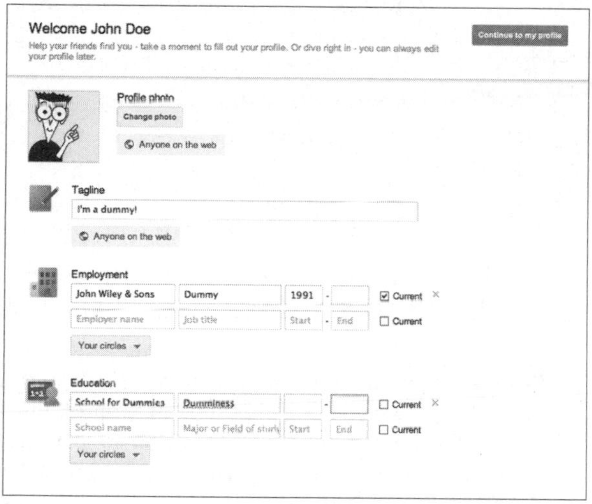

Figure 1-2: Enter even more information about yourself.

Here are the basic pieces of information that appear:

- ✔ **Tagline:** This is a simple tagline that appears below your name, telling people in a sentence or two who you are (see Figure 1-3).

- ✔ **Employment:** The more you enter here, the more likely Google+ will suggest interesting people to circle. Use this field as a way to present your resume to others. Think, "If my ideal employer were to visit my profile, which jobs would I want to show here?" You never know — maybe someone hiring might just stumble upon your profile some day and offer you a job!

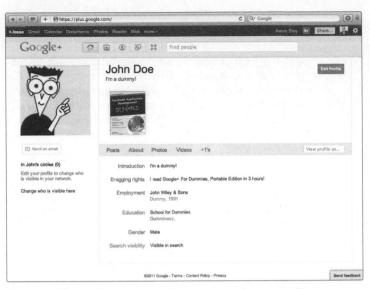

Figure 1-3: The tagline appears below your name in your profile.

✓ **Education:** This is another item that seems to get fed into the Google+ recommendation engine. If you fill out your educational background, others who attended the schools you did will show up in the recommendations that Google+ provides.

✓ **Scrapbook:** Add as many images as you like here. This is a great place to show what you look like and even reveal your personality. Feel free to be creative here. These images appear at the top of your profile below your name. These images can decorate your profile and show off your creativity!

For each option you fill out, be sure to choose the circles you want to see that information. If you don't want everyone seeing the schools you attended or have some embarrassing pictures (probably best to just leave those out, but who am I to tell you what to do?), you can adjust which circles and people will see each section you fill out in your profile.

When you click Continue to My Profile, your completed basic profile appears, which should look like Figure 1-3 (with your stuff, of course).

Setting Up Your Profile — Advanced

After you've set up your basic profile settings, you should probably go in and fill out a little more about yourself. The basic areas you'll want to fill out include your About page, your Circle settings, and the privacy options on the other tabs on your profile. I'll start by taking you through the About page.

These settings and options are likely to change over time, so be sure to check back with the Facebook Page for this book or follow me on Google+ at `http://profiles.google.com/jessestay` to be sure you're updated as things change on Google+.

Filling out your About page

Your About page is the tab on your profile that people first see when they're visiting your profile. This tab tells people more about who you are, where you're from, and anything else you feel like sharing. The options on this page are, of course, all optional, but remember that the more Google knows about you, the better recommendations Google+ can provide for you. To edit this page, go to the About page and click Edit Profile. Then click on the text you'd like to edit and it will magically turn into an edit box!

You will see two modes on your profile: Edit mode and View mode. Clicking Edit Profile takes you into Edit mode, which allows you to edit anything you click on in your profile. When you go from tab to tab in Edit mode, you can edit anything under the tabs. Click Done Editing when you want to go back to View mode.

Here are the options available to you (see Figure 1-4):

> ✔ **Introduction:** This is the first statement people see about you, so make it good! Write a paragraph or two describing what you do and what you want people to know about you.

✔ **Bragging Rights:** What is your claim to fame? Maybe you invented the Internet. Maybe you kissed Shamu the whale. This is where you can share something witty or maybe even something factual that people should know about you. Make people laugh here!

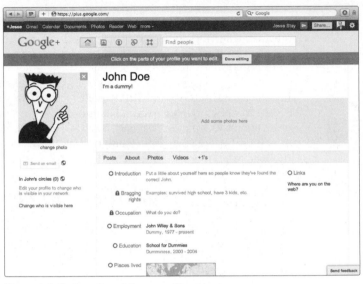

Figure 1-4: Options for editing your About page.

✔ **Occupation:** Because you filled this out before, you shouldn't need to fill it out again. If you need to add more work or perhaps you didn't complete it, now is the time to add more jobs.

✔ **Employment:** You filled this out earlier, but this is the list of jobs you have worked for in the past.

✔ **Education:** If you didn't fill this out before, add the schools you attended here so Google+ knows to recommend others who attended the same schools.

✔ **Places Lived:** Also good for Google's recommendations, this is a great way to show others where you're from or where you've lived. If you don't think this is interesting, just don't fill it out and it won't appear.

✔ **Home:** This is a great way to use your circles. Set this to a Friends and Family circle and now your close friends and family can easily find out how to contact you at home. You can add a phone number, e-mail address, postal address, fax number, and a few other options to help your friends find and contact you.

If you limit it to a specific circle, only the people in that circle will see it.

✔ **Work:** You may want this to be a little more public than your Home information so that your clients or coworkers can find you (or maybe that's a bad idea). Here you can enter a different set of information about how people can contact you at work if they need to. Just like the Home information, you can also leave this option blank if you don't want to share it with anyone (or set it to the Self circle).

✔ **Relationship:** Who knows? Maybe that special someone is on Google+ and just might find your profile and notice you're single. Or maybe you're married and it would be a bad idea to give anyone the impression that you're "on the market." Here you can choose your marital status. Google, being as diverse as it is, has a plethora of options to choose from.

✔ **Looking For:** Similar to Facebook and other social networks, here is where you can say what you're trying to get from Google+. Maybe you're using it for dating. Maybe you just want to network with others. Or you can just leave it blank and let people guess — you choose.

✔ **Gender:** This is pretty simple: male, female, or other. Some people take issue with the lack of choices in today's environment, but for now at least those are your options.

✔ **Other Names:** I anticipate this is where your pseudonym or nickname will be used in the future. If you have a maiden name, put it here. If you're known by another name (or two), put those here. Chances are that this will become more useful in the future.

✔ **Nickname:** What do you go by? This is where you can specify what everyone calls you. This item will likely become more useful as well, as Google+ begins to adapt personas and ways you can represent yourself differently to different people.

✔ **Search Visibility:** Don't want anyone to know you're on Google+? Uncheck this box and you'll remain incognito to people searching for your name. Want to keep your old high school buddies from finding you? This may be a good way to prevent that from happening.

Just as when setting up a basic profile earlier in the chapter, you can choose who sees any of the preceding options by selecting the circles to which you want those options visible. That means if you want only your closest friends and family to see your Introduction, you can do so. If you want to know more about what circles are, skip to Chapter 2 where I cover circles in more depth.

Setting your circle settings (say that five times fast!)

Under the About tab, you will find your circles in the left-hand column. These are the people you circled as well as the people who have circled you. To set who can see the people that you have circled, follow these steps:

1. **Go to the main Google+ page and click Profile; then click Edit Profile.**

   Google+ puts you in Edit mode.

2. **Click one of the lists on the left ("in Jesse's circles" or "Have Jesse in circles.")**

   A box like the one shown in Figure 1-5 appears. Here you can edit who can see who you circled and which lists will be visible to others on your profile.

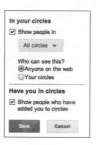

Figure 1-5: Editing Circle settings.

If you haven't circled anyone or no one has circled you, you may not see anyone in the left column! If this section seems confusing, skip to the section "Picking Whom to Follow" later in this chapter to discover how to find some people and get others to start following you. Then come back here and this section will make much more sense.

3. **Click the down arrow next to All Circles and specify which circles you want visible to those who visit your profile.**

   You can stop here if you want, or you can take it one step further though and specify who can see the circles you just chose.

4. **Click the radio button next to Your Circles and choose the circles you want the list of people you circled to be visible to.**

See how granular you can get? Keep this in mind as you get used to Google+ — you can always fine-tune your settings later.

If you don't want anyone to see the list of people you have circled, uncheck the Show People In box. Why would you want to hide this box? Well, most people have no problem just leaving this list visible to everyone; however, you may have some friends who would prefer not to be visible to others on Google+. In these cases, it may be respectful to exclude them from being visible to those visiting your profile.

You can also turn off the list of people who have circled you — maybe you just don't want to show off the number of people who have circled you. To turn that option off, just uncheck the Show People Who Have Added You to Circles box and that list won't be visible on your profile anymore.

5. **Click Save; then click Done Editing.**

Your changes are reflected in the left column of your profile.

Setting other privacy options

While in Edit mode, you will also find options on each tab of your profile. (Click Profile from your main Google+ page, click Edit Profile to get into Edit mode, and then click the name of the tab.) Here are some of the options available for each tab:

✔ **Photos:** In the Edit mode of the Photos tab (see Figure 1-6), you can do the following:

- Opt to turn off the tab by unchecking "Show this tab on your profile" so that it isn't visible on your profile. Doing so will keep others from seeing your Google+ Photos, for example (turn to Chapter 9 to learn more about the Google+ Photos integration in Google+).

- Choose who can tag photos of you — you can choose individual people or individual circles of people. This is a great way to prevent spam tagging of you in photos.

- Turn off the geo location option so people can't tell where you took the photos you store in your profile.

✔ **Videos:** With videos, you can opt to turn the Videos tab on or off by unchecking the box next to "Show this tab on your profile." In the Google+ initial release, this tab doesn't have a great deal to it.

Figure 1-6: Editing your photo visibility.

🗸 **+1s:** These are the things you've "+1d" around the web. For example, if you go to my blog StayNAlive.com (nudge, nudge), you'll see a big +1 button next to each article. Every time you click one of those +1 buttons, the website you +1d will appear on this tab. You can also click +1 next to each Google search results on Google search — every time you click, the URL you +1d will appear here. See the next section for more information on +1s.

You can opt to have these +1s appear to your friends when they visit your profile. I just leave this option checked, but you decide what you want others to see.

🗸 **Buzz:** Google Buzz, which you'll see under Buzz in Gmail, is basically the predecessor to Google+. In Buzz you can choose to automatically aggregate things like Google Reader shares and Twitter posts and other things you do around the web. If you want your Google Buzz shares to appear on your Google+ profile, just check the check box next to "Show this tab on your profile" in Edit mode on this tab and your Google Buzz shares will appear so your friends can see them.

To see your profile in its final form, click Done Editing, which takes you back to your profile. To go back to your stream, click the Google+ logo at the left of the sandbar. (Briefly, the sandbar is the narrow black bar at the top of Google+. For more on the sandbar, see the "Using the Sandbar on Other Google Products" section later in this chapter.)

Understanding the +1

There are two types of +1 buttons on Google+: +1s for websites and +1s for individual posts inside Google+. On posts inside Google+, it's like giving a person a "high five," letting them know you liked their posts. It helps search results appear more relevant on the web and Google search results (by showing you results your friends have shown interest in) and they also appear in your Google+ profile. Beyond that the +1 doesn't do a whole lot yet, but Google+ could expand the feature in the future.

The +1 is similar to a Facebook Like button, but there are two major differences at this point, including:

- ✔ On Facebook, a like subscribes you to a post's content and you get notifications for every new comment on that post. On Google+, you don't get notifications for the posts you +1.

- ✔ On Facebook like buttons for websites, while liking the website adds it to your interests in a similar manner to how Google+ adds it to your +1s tab in your profile, Facebook also allows website owners to publish content to the Facebook streams of those that have liked their website. On Google+, at least at the moment, website owners can't publish to the streams of those that have +1d their website.

Even though, compared to Facebook, the Google +1 button doesn't do much right now, you should still consider using it anyway — it's a great way to just show someone you're listening and that you like their post without doing much. And, as mentioned earlier, Google+ is also likely to expand on the functionality of the +1 button over time.

I'm asked all the time when Google+ will have a –1 button or link. If history serves right, they won't. Just like Facebook does not have a Dislike button, Google will likely not have a –1 button because –1 is, well, negative. Both Google and Facebook seem to agree that it's much better to give users a positive experience than it is to encourage a negative, and a –1 button could definitely bring negative feelings to the service.

Following Others on Google+

On Google+ a *follower* is someone who circles you. I cover this in detail in Chapter 2, so I won't go into too much detail here. However, you don't just follow every person you "follow." Instead, you *circle* them, which means you choose which circles they belong to.

Before you can get anything from the Google+ experience, you need to follow some people by adding them to your circles. In the following sections I'll show you some tips on how to get this process going.

Picking whom to follow

Now that you have your profile complete, you're ready to find some people to follow, which you can do in a few different ways:

- ✓ **Follow the recommendations.** You can start by just following the recommendations on the right side of the page (to find out how to add people to circles, see Chapter 2). Google+ chooses these based on the information you filled out in your profile, as well as those people whom you already circled and those who circled you, along with the information they filled out in their profiles.

- ✓ **Search for people.** You can start searching for people you know. Just enter names in the search bar at the top, and you'll immediately see recommendations based on those names. Or if you know their e-mail addresses, you can obtain even more accurate recommendations by just entering their e-mail address in the search bar.

✔ **Import your contacts.** You can go to your circles page via the circles icon at the top of Google+ (see Figure 1-7), and by giving Google+ some more information about your contact list (by uploading from a site like Yahoo or Hotmail) Google+ can provide more suggestions. To do so, click the little circles icon at the top of Google+, click Find People, and choose from the options provided (Yahoo, Hotmail, Upload Your Address Book, and so on). Or go with one of the people it already suggests.

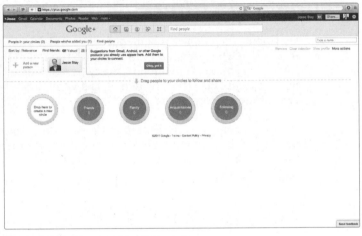

Figure 1-7: Finding new friends to circle.

Organizing your followers

Once you've picked some people to follow, you need to add them to a circle. You may want to start by going to your circles page and clicking the circle named Drop Here to Create a New Circle. Clicking that circle enables you to create a new circle and add people to it. There are then two ways to add people to a circle: Drag them to the circle in which you want them (they can be in as many circles as you like), or when you see their name in Google+, just mouse over their name and select the check boxes for the circles to which you want to add them. It's that simple! Once they are added to at least one circle, you will immediately start seeing them in your stream. You can learn more about this in Chapter 2.

Using the Sandbar on Other Google Products

The minute you start using Google+, you'll notice some new options in the upper right corner of the bar that appears across the Google products you use. In Google+, you'll see your name, followed by a red bubble with a number in it, a Share button, and an icon with your picture in it. This bar at the top of all Google products has become known as the *sandbar*. This is where you'll be notified across any Google product that there are new updates (comments, new followers, shares) to your Google+ feed. Check out Figure 1-8 to see what I'm talking about.

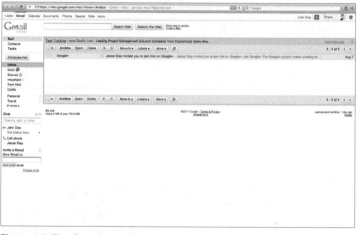

Figure 1-8: The Google sandbar.

If you're a Gmail user or a Google Reader user, you'll notice that you can also use Google+ from those products as well such that the Google+ experience follows you through every product you use on Google — and you don't even have to leave those products to use them! In any Google product, here is what you will find:

✔ **The notification bubble:** If you don't have any notifications, your bubble is gray, but as soon as you get new notifications that bubble changes to red with an animation of a white number dropping into the red box, showing the number of new notifications you have. Click this bubble, and you'll see notifications about all the new comments, shares, and new people circling you in your Google+ feed. It's addictive!

You can click the bubble even if it's gray to see old notifications.

✔ **The Share button:** You can also post to Google+, without even being in Google+! To do so, in any Google product with the sandbar installed, just click the Share button and you're presented with an option to post to Google+.

Making Your First Post

That brings me to the final, and most important, step for getting you started in Google+: your first post! Posting on Google+ is actually quite easy. However, you need to become familiar with a few things that are a bit different than social networks such as Facebook, Twitter, and others. One element you will be familiar with is posting a status update for your friends to see. I'll cover that next.

Choosing your message

If you're used to using other social networks, you should already be familiar with posting messages to your friends. Just click the Share What's New box and start entering text in the box. I recommend a message that engages your audience. Think of questions that people will want to answer or something that will get people debating. Maybe you want to share a funny graphic or video. Here are the types of things you can share:

✔ **Text:** Just start typing. That's it! If you include a link in your text, Google+ should automatically detect it as a link, and if your link points to a video, Google+ will automatically attach a video.

✔ **Graphics:** You can easily upload images from your hard drive to include in your Google+ posts. You can include static images, and Google+ also supports animated gifs as well (which you should use sparingly, depending on what your audience is interested in).

✔ **Videos:** You can either upload your own videos or link to a YouTube video. The video will be embedded right alongside your text. Google owns YouTube, so the integration is seamless.

✔ **Links:** You can attach links, and the first graphic and description for the page you linked to will automatically attach itself to your post. Google hasn't been clear on how these images and descriptions are chosen, unfortunately.

✔ **Share your location:** If your browser supports it, you can also attach the location of where you are posting alongside the status update you shared. If you include the location with your update, a little map will be attached to your post, showing where you are.

You can **bold**, *italicize*, and ~~strikethrough~~ text in Google+ if you know the syntax. To bold text, surround your text with an asterisk (*) on either side, *like this*. To italicize, surround your text with an underscore (_) on either side, _like this_. To strikethrough, surround your text with a hyphen on either side, -like this-.

Choosing your destination

The most difficult part of posting is choosing whom you want to see your post. On Facebook, you do so with a little-used (or little-known) feature called *friend lists*. Google+ uses circles to determine who can see your posts; circles are a little simpler than lists because they are in your face every step of the way and are required to choose and set up before you can even post your first status update. You may have to understand what it's doing for it to seem simpler, though.

By default, your first post will not have any circles associated with it. Google+ makes you choose which circles you want to post to. So you'll need to choose. Click Add Circles or People to Share With underneath your post. The following are all options you can choose from:

✔ **Public:** When you choose public, anyone in the world can see your post, and Google can also index it. If you're doing this for business reasons, the posts that you want to keep and remain visible to anyone should be marked as Public. Just keep in mind that everyone, even those not in your circles or even on Google+, can see it.

✔ **Your Circles:** By choosing Your Circles, only those people in the circles you have assigned people to are able to see your post. This is a great way to limit your content to just your own network.

✔ **Extended Circles:** Choosing this option makes your post visible to everyone in your own circles, in addition to everyone in those people's circles. This means the post is not quite Public, but it's getting closer!

✔ **Custom circles you created:** You can also limit your posts to just the circles you've created. For example, if I just want my post to be seen by my family members, I can select my Family circle and only my family will see my update.

✔ **Specific users or e-mail addresses:** You can also limit your post to specific users or e-mail addresses. This is a great way to choose a quick list of people to start a conversation with, or maybe to just have a one-on-one conversation with another person.

Because you can post to specific e-mail addresses, you can try a couple of different things with the updates you post. One option is to add their e-mail address to posts so that when you share to that address your post is archived in your e-mail inbox (like Gmail, for instance). Another option is to create a blank circle titled Notes, post your update to that circle, and now you have a unique way to go back and review notes you've shared!

Remember that anything you post on Google+ can be shared at a minimum to the circles and extended circles of the people you are sharing with. Never share anything you don't want to risk others sharing (or maybe you'll just want to remind them in your post that you don't want it shared, assuming you can trust them of course)!

Notifying friends who haven't circled you

By default, only those who have circled you will see your post in their stream. You'll want to use this notification feature sparingly (it could be construed as spam), but you can choose to notify people in your circles who have not circled you back and they will see your updates. To do so, select the custom circle you want to post to and then mouse over the name of the circle. A dialog box will pop up with an option to Notify About This Post. If you check that box, all those who haven't circled you will receive a notification with your post in the notification.

Be very careful forcing notifications on people! Doing so may be perceived by others as spam and will not serve you well, particularly if you do it a lot. Use this feature sparingly, unless you know your friends are okay with it!

If you like the good ol' days before the mouse when the keyboard reigned supreme, Google+ supports keyboard shortcuts, too! To go to the next message in Google+, press the J key. To go to the previous message in Google+, press the K key. To page down, press your space bar. To page up, press Shift+space bar.

Chapter 2

Boggling Over Circles and Privacy

In This Chapter

▶ Acclimating to circles

▶ Reading content from your circles

▶ Creating your own circles

*N*ow that you've submitted your first post, you may want to know a little more about who is seeing that post and how much they can actually see about you on Google+. To do this you'll need to understand more about what circles are, the various ways to create them, and how you can use them to customize who sees just about anything you can share on Google+.

In this chapter, I show you how to create and add people to circles; how to find new, interesting people to circle; and how to invite those that aren't yet on Google+ to the service. I'll also show you who can see particular circles, when notification e-mails are sent, and how to customize who sees your profile and what they can see about you.

Understanding Circles

In Google+, you don't follow or friend people, you *circle* them. Everything on the service revolves around circling people you want to follow, or applying content so that only particular circles can see that content. On Facebook, this can be compared to "friends lists," although few people know that you can do the same things with friends lists on Facebook as you can with circles (friends lists are pretty hard to find on Facebook).

 To try out Facebook friends lists, click the little drop-down arrow right next to the Post button below your status update before you post; from there you can customize the lists of people who see your post. To create new friends lists and add people to them, you'll need to click on Friends in the left column and then Manage Friend List at the top of the next page. Check out this link at Facebook's Help Center for more information about friends lists:

```
http://www.facebook.com/help/?faq=200538509990389
```

Circles play two distinct roles in Google+:

- ✓ **They help you decide whom you want to share content with.** With circles, you can choose who sees your posts. You can also use circles to target who can see certain elements of your profile as well as who can see your name in search results. Expect this to expand even further in the future as Google+ expands so that other websites can integrate circles.

- ✓ **They help you decide whose content you want to see.** You can view customized content from your circles just by clicking the circle name on the left column.

 Where are all the people you're circling? You may have joined Google+ and circled a bunch of people, but notice that you're still not seeing updates in your stream. Probably this is because those people haven't circled you yet, and they post their updates to only specific circles. Unless the people you are circling post to their Public circle, you will not see any of their content unless they add you to one of the circles they're posting content to.

 On the one hand, at times it can be beneficial to post your content publicly to ensure more people see it. On the other hand, if you *are* concerned about how many people see your content, circles can be a great way to ensure you have complete control over who sees the things you post.

Creating Circles

Now that you know what circles are, you'll probably want to dig in and start creating some! You can create circles on Google+ in a few different ways and I delve into each way in the following sections.

Dragging people into the "Drop Here to Create a New Circle" circle

To start, go to your Circles page (you can get there by clicking the little Circles button at the top of Google+ — see Figure 2-1). The Drop Here to Create a New Circle circle appears in the lower left part of your circles. Follow these steps to add someone to this circle:

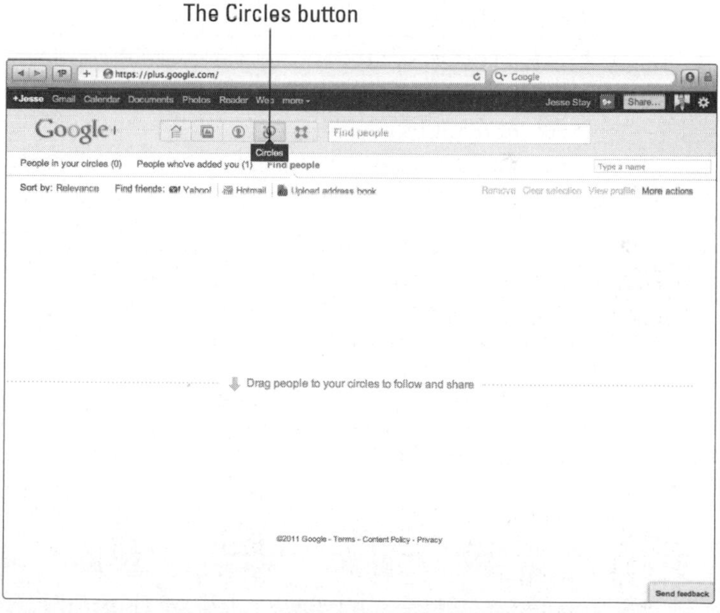

The Circles button

Figure 2-1: Click the Circles button to get to your Circles page.

1. **Click any individual you see and drag that person to the Drop Here to Create a New Circle circle.**

   The person is added to that circle and a new link appears with the words Create Circle (see Figure 2-2).

2. **Add as many more people as you like to that circle.**

   To add more people, drag them just like you did the first person.

3. **Click "Create circle."**

   A new pop-up box appears with the option to name your new circle and add even more people if you choose. Then do the following to create your circle:

   A. Name your circle

   B. Add the other people.

   C. Click Create Circle with x People. Your circle now appears with all the other circles!

Create Circle link

Figure 2-2: The Drop Here to Create a New Circle circle.

Clicking the "Drop Here to Create a New Circle" circle

When you mouse over that circle, notice that the text changes to Create Circle. If you click Create Circle, a dialog box appears. Follow the instructions in the dialog box to create your new circle.

Mousing over people's names to configure circles

In your stream, just about anywhere you see someone's name you can mouse over it and configure circles the individual belongs to (see Figure 2-3). In the pop-up dialog box that appears when you mouse over the name, you can also add new circles to assign to that individual. Just follow these steps to create a circle using this method:

1. **Mouse over the name of the individual you want to create a circle for.**

   A new pop-up box appears next to the name (see Figure 2-3). In the pop-up box, you will see either a green, rectangular box with the name of one of the circles that individual is in or the text "Add to Circles."

2. **Mouse over the green box.**

   A new pop-up box appears next to the green box.

   You can also follow steps 2 and 3 here on the profile page of any user. Look for the green box in the upper right, mouse over, and you can create a new circle there as well.

3. **Click Create Circle.**

   A text field appears.

4. In the text field that appears, name your circle and click Create.

That person is added to the new circle. Now whenever you mouse over the name and the green box you'll see a check mark next to your new circle. You can now add other people to that circle.

Figure 2-3: Mousing over the name to configure someone's circles.

Adding People to Your Circles

Now that you've created some circles, it's time to add people to those circles. You can do so exactly like you do to create your circles (as discussed in the last section):

1. Drag your friends to the circle on the Circles page.

2. Mouse over each name and check the box next to the circle you want to add each person to (see Figure 2-4).

3. **Visit the user's profile, mouse over the green circles button in the upper right, and check the boxes next to the circles you want to add them to.**

Figure 2-4: Checking the boxes next to the circles you want.

Consuming the Content for Each Circle

At this point I will assume you've created some circles, found some people to make your stream more interesting, and circled those people. If so, you're ready start consuming their content.

If you ever need to populate your stream with lots of content, feel free to follow my stream by searching for "Jesse Stay" or going to `http://profiles.google.com/jessestay`. Doing so is guaranteed to fill up your stream with all sorts of conversations that you may or may not like. I warn you though — adding a boisterous poster like me will very quickly take over the posts of anyone who posts less frequently! You may want to put me in your "noisy" circle.

In Google+, you can choose to take the default route and consume everything in every one of your circles, or consume that of a single circle. To choose a specific circle, click one of the circle links on the left (see Figure 2-5) and your stream will change to the content from that particular circle. As you can see from the figure, clicking the Wiley Editors circle on my page produces a list of Wiley editors (well, one of them — the one editing this book).

Wiley Editors circle stream

Figure 2-5: Clicking my Wiley Editors circle produces this book's Wiley editor.

It's up to you to decide which way you want to consume content. Google+ is likely to add even more filtering options in the future, so you may also have other options at some point.

Regardless, using the circles list makes reading your stream of such a diverse group of people much easier.

In Figure 2-5, under Wiley Editors, notice the Incoming and Notifications links. The Incoming link takes you to another stream view that shows updates of all the people that have circled you but that you have not circled back. This approach could be a great way not to follow everyone back while staying up with the updates of the people who have circled you. I find this stream view one of the most interesting views on Google+ because it introduces me to new people who are circling me (see Figure 2-6). The Notifications link is just the list of notifications you have received on Google+. This list includes comments, shares, and new people who have circled you, among other things. If you miss a notification from your sandbar notification, just come here and you can catch up on everything (see Figure 2-7).

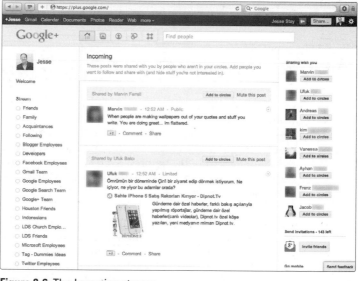

Figure 2-6: The Incoming stream.

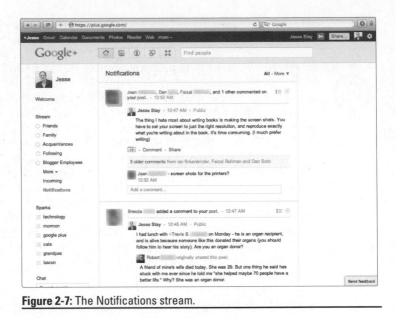

Figure 2-7: The Notifications stream.

Inviting New People to Google+

Google+ initially launched as an invite-only beta environment, which meant that your friends could use Google+ only if you invited them. Google seems to change their rules on inviting people frequently though, and lo and behold after about nine weeks in closed beta they released Google+ to the masses, dubbing the new service in "open beta," which is where it is at the time of this writing.

Because invitations are no longer required, Google+ no longer limits the number of invitations it gives users like it did in the first week or so. You can see the Invite Friends button displayed in the right-hand column of your stream view (see Figure 2-8). Simply click that link to invite someone to Google+.

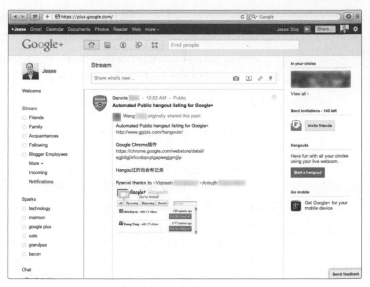

Figure 2-8: Click Invite Friends to invite them to Google+.

You can invite friends one of two ways: invite them by e-mail or share a link that they can click. Here's how you invite them by e-mail:

1. **In the right column of your stream view, click Invite Friends.**

   A new pop-up box appears, prompting you to invite your friends.

2. **Click Add More People to Invite.**

   This link accesses a text box where you type e-mail addresses of friends you want to invite. Add as many e-mail addresses as you like. As you type each e-mail address, a drop-down box appears with their e-mail address. Select it.

3. **Click the input box and type the next e-mail address.**

4. **When you're done, click Send Email.**

   The people you invited will receive an invitation to join Google+ via an e-mail from you.

Here's how you invite them with just a link:

1. **In the right column of your stream view, click Invite Friends.**

   When you click this button, a new pop-up box appears prompting you to invite your friends.

2. **Copy and paste the link in the pop-up box.**

   At the bottom of the pop-up box, you'll be given a link. Just copy that link and paste it into a Facebook status update, Twitter post, or e-mail to share it with your friends. With the link, it's first come, first served until your number is up, so tell your friends to act fast!

Setting Who Can See Your Profile

Just as with your status updates, using circles you can customize how people see elements of your profile. I cover this in detail in Chapter 1. To reiterate, next to each option on the Edit mode of your profile (remember, you get there by clicking Edit Profile), you can assign a circle that can see that information. When you assign that piece of information on your profile to a given circle, only the people in that circle will be able to see that given element of your profile. This can be a great way to share a phone number or e-mail address with only your closest friends and family, for example.

As an example, do just that. Assume that you created a Family circle (currently, that is actually already created for new users of Google+). To set it so your phone number is only visible to family, do this:

1. **Click the Profile button at the top of Google+ (see Figure 2-9). You can also just click your name on your stream view.**

   This takes you to your profile page.

Profile button

Figure 2-9: The profile button at the top of Google+.

2. **Click the Edit Profile button in the upper right of your profile.**

   You are taken to the Edit mode of your About tab, where you can edit any piece of the page.

3. Go down to Home (it highlights a purplish color) and click on it.

A new pop-up box appears (see Figure 2-10), allowing you to add or edit a home phone number and other information.

Figure 2-10: Adding a phone number in Google+.

4. Add your phone number.

Make sure Phone is selected in the drop-down box and enter your phone number in the text box provided.

5. Set the circles you want to see that number.

By default, this is set to Anyone on the Web. You'll want to do the following:

A. Click the drop-down box and select Custom.

A new dialog box appears that looks a lot like the circles dialog box you encountered when you were creating and adding people to circles earlier in this chapter.

B. Click the "X" next to Public.

C. Click the Add More People link and check the box next to your Family circle.

D. Click the "Save" button in the dialog box and you're done!

6. Click "Done editing."

Once you do so, no one but your family will be able to see your home phone number. Try this out now with other elements of your profile!

Be careful what you share! Even though you are limiting your content to a specific circle or group of people, there is nothing stopping those individuals from sharing your post with their circles and extended circles or even just taking a screen shot. Just as in real life, make sure you always trust the friends you share with, and even if you do, consider simply not posting anything embarrassing! Social networks are a lot like high school — after one rumor gets going, they're pretty hard to stop! Better to not give any fodder that could cause such rumors to spread.

Chapter 3

Posting to Google+

● ●

In This Chapter

▶ Deciding what to post and who to post to

▶ Knowing who to share to

▶ Knowing what you can share

▶ Moderating your posts

▶ Getting comments on your posts

● ●

*I*n Chapter 1, you create your first post on Google+. You also find out how to post to Google+ and get the post out to the circles you choose.

In this chapter, you dive deeper into posting, using tips I suggest to post things that are engaging, that will get comments, and that will target the audiences you're looking for. I also give you some tips on how you can further target your audience and determine the best methods to write good content that meets the needs of that audience. Lastly, I cover how you can moderate your posts, remove comments, block users, ignore users, and even how to deal with nagging users and trolls.

Knowing What to Post

To get off and running on Google+, your first step is to choose something engaging to post. The term *engaging* is key — engaging means content that gets people commenting, sharing, +1ing, and talking about your post. In the following sections I suggest several strategies you can use to make your posts appealing.

When you +1 a post on Google+, it's like "high-fiving" the individual that wrote the post, and the person who wrote the post can see that you +1d it. It's a compliment to the person writing to have someone +1 their post. Beyond that, +1ing a post really doesn't do much else on Google+ at the time I write this.

Sharing posts with only close friends and family

Believe it or not, this is one of the most common uses of social networking sites such as Facebook. I have an idea that this is why you came to try out Google+. If so, you'll need to do a few things to ensure that you're getting what you want from Google+:

- ✔ **Make sure your close friends and family have Google+ accounts and are using them.** This should be your first task. If you can't convince your close friends and family to use Google+, you may be sorely disappointed! Try inviting them by sending them personalized invite e-mails (which you do by sending them an e-mail with the invite link I mention in Chapter 2). You can also refer them to this book so they can find out why they might want to use Google+.

  In the end, if you are on Google+ because you want to share better with your close friends and family and your close friends and family simply won't join, you may end up deciding Google+ isn't for you. That's okay! You can find just as much benefit from other tools, such as Facebook.

- ✔ **Post content your close friends and family will understand!** If you're posting for your close friends and family, or you want them to get more involved on the site, don't post content they're not going to understand. For example, I enjoy technology. My family doesn't understand a lot about technology. As a result, if I want my family to be involved in my posts, I'm not going to post a lot of tech-related posts to my Family circle.

If you want to involve a personal audience, post personal updates!

Be careful posting anything *too* personal on Google+! If you want to share more personal updates, you may want to consider posting them just to a Close Friends or Family circle. If it's *really* personal, consider not posting at all — remember, even with circles, anyone can still share what you post to their circles and extended circles!

✔ **Create circles specifically for these groups if you will be posting other types of content.** You may want to consider creating a Family circle or Close Friends circle just for targeting updates to your close friends and family. For example, whenever I post pictures of my children, I always post them to my Close Friends circle and not to the public or other circles. This ensures the privacy and safety of my children, but also keeps my close friends and family receiving a more targeted stream than my normal stream.

✔ **Post less frequently to these circles of friends and family.** I've found that my close friends and family don't like to see too many updates. I've had close friends and family uncircle me (I never take it personally) just because my stream is typically noisy. If you are on Google+ mostly for friends and family, consider their streams — do you want to be the only one dominating their stream, or do you want to leave room for others?

Also, keep in mind that many of your close friends and family won't be as familiar with how to use Google+ (remember to share this book with them!), so even as Google+ gets better filtering for this type of stuff (such as the ability to filter out all the posts with the word "cat" in them, for example), there's a chance they don't know how to use it. You don't have to post less frequently to please your close friends and family, but if your main purpose is to communicate with your close friends and family, you may want to consider it.

Posting to journal your life

This is one way to post that actually got me started in social media; Google+, Facebook, and other social media sites are great places to keep a running journal of your life, what you're doing, and how you're succeeding. Follow these tips if you want to use Google+ to journal:

- ✔ Focus on accomplishments, not everyday tasks (like what you ate for lunch).

- ✔ Be sure that if you're sharing to the world and remain focused on things in your life that people might find interesting.

- ✔ Consider posting journal-type entries you don't want the world to see to a circle (maybe name it, well, *Journal*) with just your e-mail address in it. This way you get a copy sent to your e-mail. You can also go back to that circle on the left of your stream and review your accomplishments.

Posting to communicate with specific groups

If you have a user group — let's say you're a photographer — you might consider creating a circle (named *Photographers*) for that group. Share the members of the photographers circle with your Google+ stream so they can also add your photographer friends to their own similar circles. Then, you can keep a tight-knit relationship with those photographers you associate with.

Think hard before posting to only a specific circle. Could others following you benefit from this post? Are other photographers outside your circle following you; if so, can you add them to your circle? Or you may want to consider just posting to your Public circle. Posting only to a specific circle can cause many, who otherwise could benefit, to not see your post.

Posting to increase the number of people circling you

Popular marketer and blogger Guy Kawasaki, author of the book *Enchantment: The Art of Changing Hearts, Minds, and Actions* (Portfolio, 2011) said, "There are only two kinds of Twitter users: those that want more followers and those that lie." (Check out `http://blog.guykawasaki.com/2008/12/how-to-use-twit.html` for more.)

Truth be told, we all care about numbers. Having lots of people care about you feels good. There's a good chance you're trying to figure out how to get more people reading your posts. Here are some tips to help increase their number:

- ✔ **Post content about things you're passionate about. Don't post content you're not passionate about.** What you write about will attract an audience that shares your particular interests. You'll attract an even larger audience if people believe you really care about the things you're writing about and if they think they are learning something.

- ✔ **Consider posts with questions or a call to action.** If you're asking your audience a question, there's a good likelihood that they'll answer. They'll also share it with their friends, perhaps causing them to answer and circle you.

- ✔ **Post interesting stuff.** I've found that funny pictures and videos tend to be shared a lot. Try thought-provoking statements that intrigue people. The more you get them to think, the more they'll comment and circle you.

- ✔ **Seek out influential folks with large audiences and tag them when you're posting something interesting.** This is how I got into blogging. I would write in response to what other bloggers were writing and link back to them, getting their attention in the process. As I wrote interesting stuff, they noticed and eventually started reading my blog and linking back to me. You can do the same in your Google+ posts through *tagging*.

Be careful that you don't tag people too much! Tagging (I cover this in Chapter 7 if you want to skip there for a quick primer) *on occasion,* especially if your topic is relevant to the people you're tagging, is okay. However, if you tag them too much, they may block you and be much less likely to circle you and follow your content in the future. Always think about whether tagging an individual in your post is truly something of interest to the individual.

If you're trying to build an audience, consider always posting to the public and using specific circles as the exception. If you post only to specific circles, people viewing your profile to see what you post won't see updates if you haven't circled them because they are only allowed to see content designated for the circles they are in. If you post to the public, anyone who wants to circle you can see your updates and can have further reason to circle you because you didn't limit your content to any one audience. Posting to your Public circle will also help you build relationships with people you haven't met, extending the potential circles you're in.

Picking Your Audience

Now that you know what to post, it's time to figure out whom to post to. You can post to different types of people and groups to ensure that your content is shared exactly the way you want.

Posting to circles

I've covered this pretty thoroughly in Chapter 2, which explains how to create and add people to circles. When you choose a circle, your post is visible only to that circle.

Keep in mind that even though you're posting to a specific circle, only the people you've circled will see the post. To be sure that everyone you're targeting in the circle sees your post, mouse over the circle name after you enter it in the Add More People box, and a new pop-up dialog box will appear (see Figure 3-1). Just check the box next to Notify About This Post, and now everyone in that circle will receive a notification about your post. Be sure you're not spamming them when you do this, though! If people believe you're spamming, they may very well block your posts.

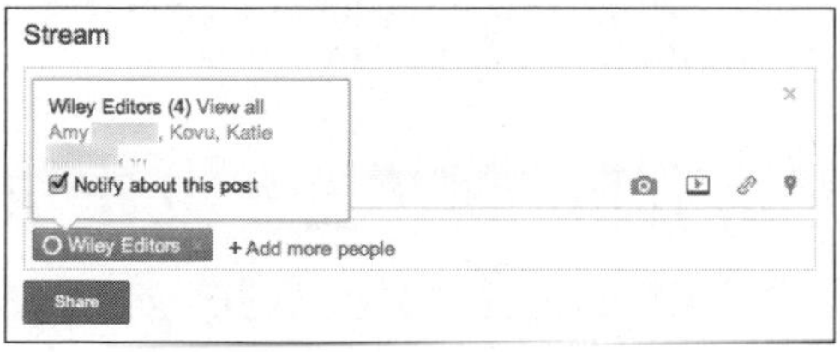

Figure 3-1: Checking Notify About This Post to notify everyone in a circle.

Posting to individuals

In addition to circles, you can post to individual members of Google+. To post to an individual, type the person's name rather than the name of a circle. To send to multiple individuals, add more individual names just like you do when posting to multiple circles (see Figure 3-2).

Figure 3-2: Entering the names of individuals to post to specific people.

To enter a name, always start by entering a plus (+) sign. This is a good habit — with this method, you can also tag people in posts.

Posting to e-mail addresses

What if the individual isn't on Google+? Or what if you can't find them? Just type an e-mail address in place of the individual's name or a circle name and an e-mail will be sent to that e-mail address with the content of your post.

Knowing who will see your posts and how they'll see the posts

You can check any time to see how others will view your posts and your profile information. To see how others can see your profile and posts, follow these steps:

1. **Go to your profile page.**

   To get there you can either click on your name in the upper left or click on the profile icon at the top.

2. **Click View Profile As.**

   You'll see this link in the upper right in the grayish bar with links to your About page, Buzz, Photos, and so on. After you click it a text box appears.

3. **Enter the name of a specific individual or a circle.**

   A drop-down menu . . . drops down.

4. **Select the same individual or circle as you did in Step 3.**

5. **Click through each part of your profile to see how that individual or circle is seeing your profile and click on Posts to see which of your posts they're seeing.**

6. **Click Done at the top to go back to your profile.**

Sharing, Resharing, and Commenting on Posts

To share a link, click the link icon in the post box. You can also paste the link inside your post to automatically attach a link to your post (see Figure 3-3).

Figure 3-3: Sharing a link on Google+.

To share an image, click the image icon in the post box. You can then choose to upload a new image, or if you're on a phone, upload from your phone's camera (see Figure 3-4).

Resharing others' posts

To reshare other friends' posts, click the Share button under the post (see Figure 3-5). A new pop-up box appears, allowing you to add your comments to their post. Again, add something engaging that gets people commenting, and post it to your stream. This can be a great way to get people commenting and circling you!

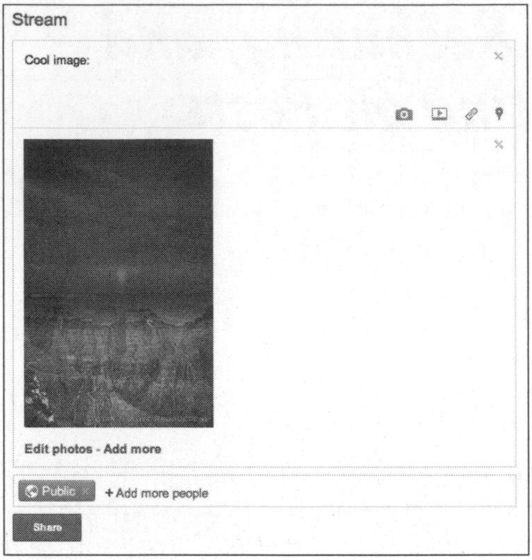

Stream

Cool image:

Edit photos - Add more

Public   + Add more people

Share

Figure 3-4: Sharing an image on Google+.

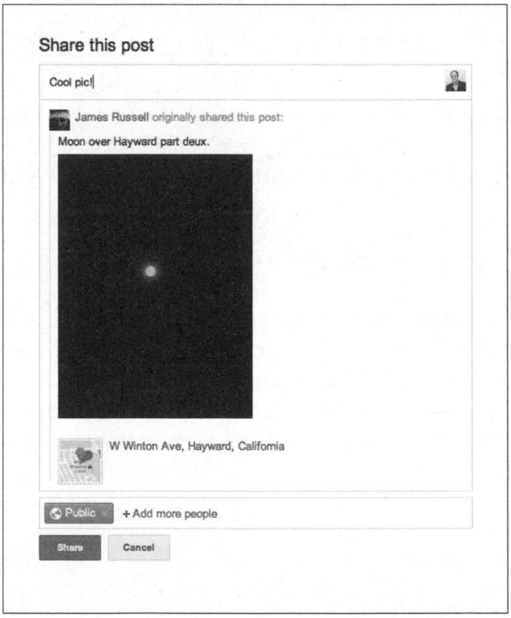

Share this post

Cool pic!

James Russell originally shared this post:

Moon over Hayward part deux.

W Winton Ave, Hayward, California

Public   + Add more people

Share   Cancel

Figure 3-5: Clicking Share to share a friend's post.

To get to the original post of a person that is being reshared, there is no *permalink* (a unique link) back to the original post. Instead, you have to click on the original poster's name and find the post in their stream. Daunting, I know, but until Google+ fixes this (maybe by the time you read this they will), this is the only way to do it!

Getting people to comment on your posts

This brings me to a question I often hear: "How can I get people commenting on my posts?" If someone joins Google+, and it's quiet, usually it's because they're not circling the right people or posting the right content. Other times it's because they're not getting people to circle you (refer to the "Posting to increase the number of people circling you" section earlier in the chapter). Here are some quick tips for getting more comments:

- ✔ Create engaging, thought-provoking posts that entice people to comment (questions are always great).

- ✔ Comment, and comment often, on others' posts. They'll remember you and start to respond (assuming your comments are engaging).

- ✔ Follow interesting people and share their content. Tag them with your thoughts on the content and end with a question.

Mentioning others in posts and comments

Replying to people in a comment thread on Google+ is easy. Just start by typing a "+" (plus) sign and then start typing their name. A drop-down list appears allowing you to select their name. Then type your comment in response to the name and they'll get a notification that you mentioned them. You can use this technique almost any time you want to bring attention to someone else on Google+.

Moderating Your Posts

It won't be long before you get a spammer or troll commenting on your posts. The bigger Google+ gets, the more spammers you'll start to see. This is especially true on public posts — spammers see this as an opportunity to generate links back to their websites, increasing search engine optimization rankings.

Search engine optimization (or SEO) is the process of ranking your website high in search engines, and there are all kinds of techniques for doing so. One of the most prominent ways is to get as many links as you can throughout the web back to your website (which I don't recommend, unless it's others, not you, linking back to your website).

Moderation is the process of managing these spammers or trolls on your posts. In the following sections, I cover some common ways you can moderate your posts if they ever get out of hand.

Editing your posts

Make a mistake? Here's how you can edit your posts:

1. **Click the triangle located in the upper right corner of your post (see Figure 3-6).**

   A drop-down menu appears.

2. **Choose Edit This Post and edit the post as you want.**

3. **Click Save.**

   Your edited post appears. The post is marked as edited so that people know it's not the original post.

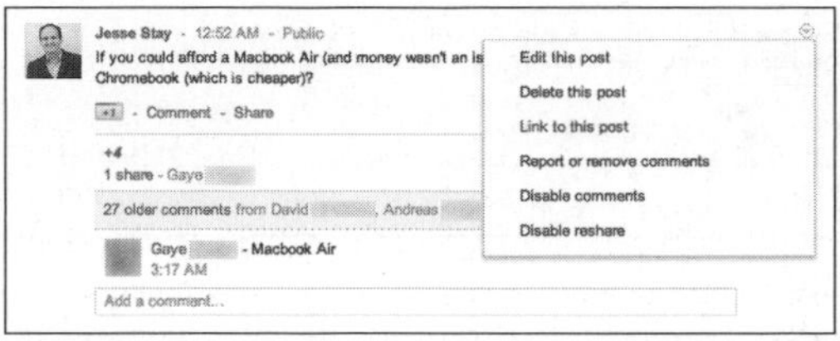

Figure 3-6: Selecting the triangle in the upper right corner to edit the post.

Deleting your posts

Deleting your post is easy. Just click the little triangle in the upper right corner of the post and select Delete This Post. You may be prompted to confirm your choice. Once you confirm, the post is gone!

Muting posts

You may have a post you don't want to see anymore. Maybe it's offensive. Maybe you're just not interested. Maybe the comments notifications are getting irritating. Whatever the case, to mute a post, click the little triangle in the upper right corner of the post and select Mute This Post and it disappears from your stream never to be seen again (unless you unmute the post, which you can do by just clicking "unmute" at any time).

Deleting comments

You can delete two types of comments: your own comments and comments to your posts by other users. For your comments, just click the Edit link below your comment, and then click the Delete Comment button in the resulting dialog box (see Figure 3-7).

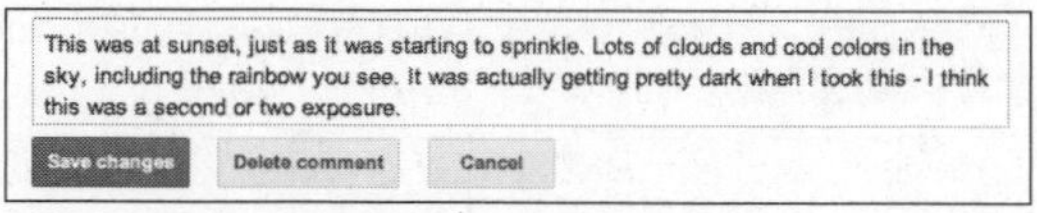

This was at sunset, just as it was starting to sprinkle. Lots of clouds and cool colors in the sky, including the rainbow you see. It was actually getting pretty dark when I took this - I think this was a second or two exposure.

Save changes   Delete comment   Cancel

Figure 3-7: Deleting your own comment.

Deleting someone else's comment is a little more complicated. Follow these steps:

1. **Click the little arrow in the upper right corner of the post with the comment you want to delete (see Figure 3-8).**

2. **Click Report or Remove Comments.**

   Little "x" buttons and flag buttons appear next to each comment.

3. **Click the "x" next to the comment you want to delete.**

   The comment disappears from view, never to be seen again!

Figure 3-8: Deleting someone else's comment.

Disabling comments or reshares

You can also disable comments on posts. This can be a great way to prevent a controversial topic from getting out of hand. Or maybe you don't want your post to be shared by anyone else. Here's how to do either one:

1. **Click the little triangle icon in the upper right corner of your post.**

2. **To disable comments, select Disable comments. To disable reshares of your post, select Disable Reshare.**

 You can actually create a make-shift poll by disabling comments on your post! To do so, just ask a multiple-choice question, add each potential answer as a separate comment, and then disable comments. Ask your audience to +1 their favorite answer, and now you have a way to get your audience voting on your posts just like a poll question!

Dealing with Trolls

Although in children's fantasy literature, a troll is one of those mean ogres who sits at the bridge not allowing anyone through, on Google+ and other social networks, a *troll* is someone who constantly criticizes just to criticize, constantly nags, and never gives up. They comment over and over with negative things and won't go away. In a way, we should really call them "gnats!"

Handling trolls short of blocking them

I recognize you're probably not a troll (although I do have a pretty big nose). However, what do you do when others troll on your posts? How should you react? You generally have three options when dealing with trolls: You can uncircle them, ignore them, or you can block them. *Uncircling* people means you won't see their posts, but they can still see yours and comment on the posts you reveal to the public. *Ignoring* the person simply removes all of their notifications from your stream and removes their updates from your Incoming stream (accessible via the left-hand column of Google+), whereas *blocking* them goes further and also prevents them from interacting with or commenting on your posts.

Here are some tips to help you react appropriately when others are trolling on your posts if you haven't quite decided to flat-out ignore or block them:

- ✔ **Begin by uncircling or ignoring.** If there isn't too much threat, just uncircle the individual and they'll only be able to comment on posts you make public. You won't have to see their posts anymore in your stream. If you really want to block them, just see the "Blocking trolls when you've just had enough" section at the end of this chapter.

- ✔ **Give trolls a "three strikes and you're out" rule.** Let's face it. Some people just have a bad day. Give them a chance. If they troll you once or even twice, let it go and just ignore them. If they troll three times or more, though, it might be worth finding a way to remove them from future conversations.

- ✔ **Don't feed the trolls!** If they truly are trolling, don't continue the trolling by arguing with them or giving them food to continue trolling with. Just politely ignore them and continue the conversation.

No one ever gets a notification that they were blocked, uncircled, or ignored. They may figure it out (especially if blocked), but they won't be notified by Google+.

Ignoring trolls when you just want a little peace and quiet

If someone is sending you a lot of notifications or tagging you a lot, you can avoid offending them with a flat-out block and still allow them to comment on your posts by ignoring them. For example, you might like browsing your Incoming stream but you want to avoid people who post a lot of profane or vulgar posts without blocking them. *Ignoring* a user is a great way to no longer receive notifications from them without being so brutal as to block them. It also removes their

updates from your Incoming stream (the stream of updates
from all the people who circled you on Google+). This means
they can still comment on your posts, share your posts, and
+1 your posts, but you won't be bothered as they do so (but
you will see their comments).

The *Incoming stream* streams updates from all the people that
have circled you on Google+ but that you have not necessarily
circled back. It's a great way to gauge who is circling you and
perhaps find some new people to circle back!

Ignoring only works for users you do not have circled who you
don't want bothering you with noisy notifications. After you
ignore them, even if they tag you or target a post to you, you'll
no longer get notifications from them, nor will you get updates
from them in your Incoming stream. If you want to ignore an
individual that you've already circled, you'll have to uncircle
them first.

To ignore someone, there are relatively few ways to make
this happen. The best way to do this as I write this is to do
the following:

1. **Uncircle the individual if necessary.**

2. **In your notifications, click on the list of new people
   that have added you to circles.**

   You may have to click View All in the upper right of
   the page to find it.

   Next to each person's name you'll see an Ignore link.

   You can reach your notifications via a link on the left
   side of your Google+ profile or by the notifications
   bubble in your sandbar at the top of your page.

3. **Click Ignore.**

   The user will be removed from your stream and your
   notifications unless you unignore them in the future.

Blocking trolls when you've just had enough

Blocking a user means that user can never see your updates again in their stream. They also can't tag you in posts. I personally don't block lightly. I block users only if they just won't leave you alone, are truly spammers, have done something that causes me to feel threatened in some way, or if I don't know them and they've trolled me enough to get on my nerves. Sometimes it's worth just getting you out of their sight and out of their mind. Blocking users helps to accomplish this in a much more extreme way than just ignoring them.

I generally avoid blocking people I know in person. If I know them in person, I will try to approach them in private first; then if I'm willing to break the friendship, I'll block them.

If they continue posting in their own stream complaining about how you blocked them, don't continue that argument. Just ignore it and let it happen. They will eventually give up and let it go.

To block a user, do the following:

1. **Go to the user's profile page.**

   You'll see the user's profile and stream.

2. **Scroll down below the list of circles in the left column and click Block *(username)*.**

   You can also report them for spam by clicking the Report and Block button instead of the Block button (see Figure 3-9).

   The user should now appear blocked (indicated by a bubble saying "Blocked" in the upper right corner of their profile). You'll never see them in your stream, and they'll never see you in their stream.

As I write this, posts marked Public in your stream will still be visible to people you have blocked. They may not be able to comment on those posts, but they can still read them. So be careful not to post anything as Public that you would not want someone you have blocked to see.

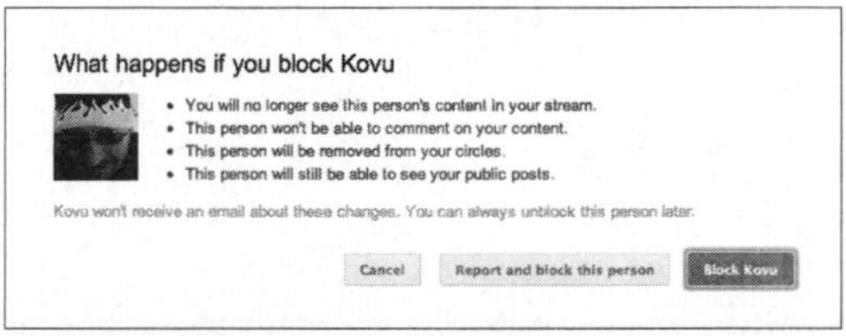

What happens if you block Kovu

- You will no longer see this person's content in your stream.
- This person won't be able to comment on your content.
- This person will be removed from your circles.
- This person will still be able to see your public posts.

Kovu won't receive an email about these changes. You can always unblock this person later.

Cancel   Report and block this person   Block Kovu

Figure 3-9: Your author about to block ... his editor?!

Chapter 4

Hanging Out with Friends

● ●

In This Chapter

▶ Starting a hangout

▶ Understanding the parts of hangouts

● ●

*M*any people are familiar with Skype and other similar video services: You send a person a Skype message and immediately you can chat with them, over video, across the world. Skype provides you with a personal way to chat with someone remotely, as though you were there in person.

Google+ has provided its users with a similar type of service called *hangouts* that allow any person to chat over a video connection with up to ten people anywhere in the world. The cool part is that Google+ doesn't charge a dime for this service.

In this chapter I show you how to start up a hangout and begin a chat with anyone in your circles on Google+.

Using hangouts requires you to have a webcam attached to your computer. This chapter is written with the assumption that you have a webcam and it is properly set up for your computer. If you need help setting up your webcam, you may want to contact your computer's manufacturer or the manufacturer of your webcam to get it working with your computer.

Starting Your First Hangout

To start your hangout, you need to click the Start a Hangout button on the right column of Google+ (see Figure 4-1). A pop-up window appears that has your video in it where you can start preparing for your hangout.

Hangouts

Have fun with all your circles using your live webcam.

Start a hangout

Figure 4-1: To start your hangout at any time, click the Start a Hangout button.

Getting your video "just right"

The pop-up window mentioned in the preceding section includes a video that you can use to check to be sure everything is set up correctly. You'll want to follow these tips before starting:

- Comb your hair. Put some clothes on (please!). Make sure you're presentable!

- Click Mute Video or Mute Mic at the bottom of the hangout configuration screen if you don't want others to see you or hear you (or both).

- Click Settings (also at the bottom of the hangout configuration screen) if you need to configure your video to pull from a different video source or choose a different microphone.

- Consider lighting — turn on the lights so it isn't too dark where you are. Open the shades. A well-lit video always looks good.

Picking whom to hangout with

Now that your video is set up and you are presentable, you need to decide who should be in your video (see Figure 4-2).

You can invite just one other person, ten specific people (Google+ only allows ten people in a hangout at a time), or an entire circle. Here are some tips to consider when deciding who can be in your video:

Figure 4-2: Choosing the people you would like to hangout with.

Hangouts have a limit of ten people per hangout. If you specify a circle with more than ten people, the first ten people to accept your invitation will be allowed in the hangout; the rest can only watch. It's first come, first served. It is also unclear if Google will ever lift the limit of ten per hangout, so when you read this, that limit could potentially be higher.

✔ Specifying individual names means each person will get a notification saying they were invited to your hangout.

✔ Specifying a circle means that the people in that circle will see you're having a hangout, but this doesn't mean they'll be notified.

✔ Specifying a hangout as Public means that it will appear in the streams of everyone who has circled you, whether they are in a circle or not. Also, your hangout can potentially appear in Google search results and other apps in the future.

✔ Choosing Your Circles means that your hangout will appear in the streams of just the people you've circled. You can, of course, be more specific by choosing only a single circle or two.

Now click Hangout and your hangout will begin.

Administering Your Hangout

Once your hangout begins, you can start having fun with it! Here are a few things you can do in your hangout (see Figure 4-3):

✔ **Invite more friends.** Click the Invite button at the bottom of the hangout window and choose the people or circles you want to invite.

✔ **Text chat with members of the hangout.** In addition to chatting over video, you can click the Chat button at the bottom of the hangout window to access a chat dialog box that allows you to text chat with members of the hangout. This approach can be useful if someone's audio isn't working, for example.

✔ **Watch a YouTube video with your friends.** By clicking the YouTube button at the bottom, you can search for any video on YouTube and watch it with all your friends in the hangout. Any member can turn off the YouTube video when they want to. This is also a great way for a family to watch a family video together even while living in different locations around the world.

✔ **Mute others in the hangout.** You can mute anyone in the hangout at any time by clicking the little speaker icon over their video feed at the bottom of the hangout window. You can also mute your own video or audio with the links at the bottom. Keep in mind that if others mute you, you can always turn your audio back on! Muting others' audio doesn't mean their audio is off forever, unfortunately.

Figure 4-3: Your author and his wife hanging out.

Chapter 5

Finding Content with Sparks

In This Chapter

▶ Choosing and creating sparks

▶ Reading and sharing your sparks

Google+ has a unique and interesting way of finding, identifying, and sharing new content that you're interested in called *sparks*. The purpose of this feature is to provide, or spark, new ideas or content you can share with your friends on Google+. In this chapter I show you how to get the most out of sparks.

Picking Your Sparks

Choosing your sparks is simple. You can choose any topic you like. If I like bacon (I eat bacon, cold, as a snack and in any form I can get it!), I can add a "bacon" spark that will provide me with news about bacon. I can then share that content with my friends on Google+. Pick the things of most interest to you.

To get started with sparks, following these steps:

1. **Click the Sparks link in the left column of your main stream on Google+.**

   The sparks search page appears (see Figure 5-1).

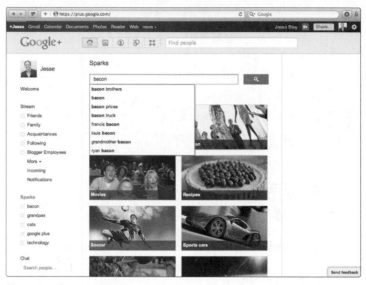

Figure 5-1: Sparks central.

2. **Choose one of the featured sparks or search for something of interest to you.**

3. **Review the content of the spark and click the Add Interest button to add the spark to the list of Sparks in the left column (see Figure 5-2).**

4. **Click the spark on the left to read its content.**

5. **Repeat Steps 1 through 4 to add more sparks to your list.**

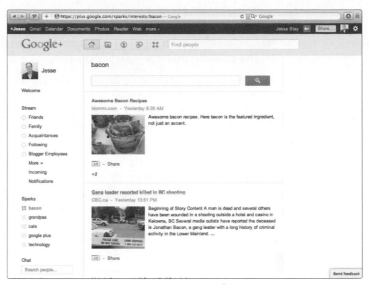

Figure 5-2: Your list of sparks appears in the left column of Google+.

Reading and Interacting with Sparks

After you add a few sparks you'll want to start using them. To read a spark, click the spark in the left-hand column of Google+. Immediately a stream of results will appear related to that spark on Google+.

Sparks gets its content from Google search results. If you want your content to appear on the Sparks stream, be sure you're exercising proper search engine optimization (SEO) techniques! Search `Dummies.com` for some great books on the topic of SEO.

Here are a few things you can do with sparks:

- ✔ **Read them!** Click the link of any spark to read the spark on the website that the spark links to.

- ✔ **Vote on them.** Click the +1 button directly beneath the spark to show your interest. The number of +1s indicates the popularity of the spark, which gives you one way to decide whether a spark is worth reading.

- ✔ **Share them with friends.** To share a spark with friends, click the Share link and a Share dialog box pops up, similar to what you would see if you were sharing on your Google+ stream (see Figure 5-3). Add a comment that will appear with the spark. Select the circle(s) or people you want to share with and click Share. The spark will now appear in your Google+ stream with all your other content!

Share this post

Awesome Bacon Recipes
blommi.com

Awesome bacon recipes. Here bacon is the featured ingredient, not just an accent.

Shared from Sparks

Public + Add more people

Share   Cancel

Figure 5-3: Clicking the Share button invokes this share dialog box.

At the time of this writing, sparks is a pretty simple tool that makes it easy to share content. It is only available via the web interface and not in any mobile app. Sparks is likely to improve over time, so pay attention to see whether Google+ adds anything new to this feature down the road. Feel free to go to this book's Facebook Page at https://www.facebook.com/googleplusportable if you have any questions.

Chapter 6

Gaming with Google+

● ●

In This Chapter

▶ Picking a game to *fiend* over

▶ Inviting others to play with you

● ●

*G*oogle+ isn't all business, and it's not just for geeky early adopters! It's also for that time you need a break, or just need to cool down. For that reason, Google+ provides a cool section called Google+ Games that allows you to find, play, and challenge your friends to games that have been built for Google+. Google+ games are much more than that, though — they're a great social way to challenge your abilities against the abilities of your friends, family, and coworkers and build relationships in the process.

In this chapter I show you how to find games you can enjoy, and how to get your friends involved in playing them with you. I warn you — these games are addictive!

Finding Games to Play

To get to Google+ Games, just click the Games icon (see Figure 6-1) at the top of your main Google+ page. The Featured Games page appears. On this page, you'll see a list of featured games followed by a stream of games your friends on Google+ are playing (If you've skipped to this chapter because you really like games and that's all you can think about right now, I encourage you to at least read Chapter 2 to learn how to add new friends and use "circles" on Google+.)

Figure 6-1: The Games icon located at the top of Google+.

You now can pick a game to play by searching and choosing the game of your preference. You can find games several ways:

- ✔ **Surf through the Featured Games.** This is the most obvious choice because these are games Google has picked to appear on the Featured Games page. On the main page of Google+ Games, you'll find graphics representing featured games that Google+ has carefully selected for you. Pick one that seems interesting. Google+ also shows you how many of your friends have played each of the games.

- ✔ **Click All Games.** If the featured games aren't enough for you, go to the left column and click All Games. A list of all the games available appears, as shown in Figure 6-2. Just hover your mouse over the avatar of the game you are interested in and a blue Play button appears; click it to play that game.

Figure 6-2: The All Games page on Google+ Games.

✔ **Browse through your Games stream.** The main Google+ Games page shows a stream of all the games your friends are playing. Browse through this list to see what might be interesting. The most popular games are probably the ones that you and your friends will find most challenging. So, pick the games that your closest friends are playing for the best experience! See the next section for more information.

✔ **Respond to Notifications.** As I discuss in the "Challenging Your Friends" section at the end of the chapter, you can invite your friends and circles to play the games you're playing. To see who has invited you to play a game, just click the Notifications link in the left column of Google+ Games and a list will be presented of those that have asked you to play with them (see Figure 6-3). The people who have invited you to play with them are people who really want to get you to try out the game with them or try out something new. It might be a fun challenge to meet their invitation!

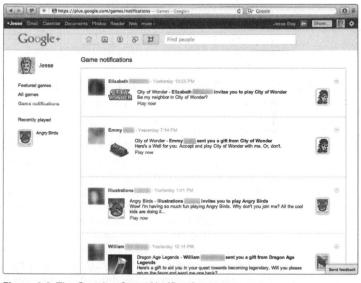

Figure 6-3: The Google+ Game Notifications page.

Each game you play can be a team-building exercise! Find games that your colleagues or family members or other types of team members may be enthusiastic about. Find ways to induce a competitive spirit among those you play with.

Reading the Games Stream

As mentioned earlier, the main page of Google+ Games includes a stream of updates from the games your friends are playing on Google+. These updates are generated automatically by each game as a way to tell your friends your progress in the game and cannot be controlled by the user. They only appear in the games stream and not your main Google+ stream, however. Browse these and notice that you can share and comment on each post. Use the following tips as you try to interact with those playing each game:

✔ **Use a games post as a conversation starter.** Google+ Games are a great way to build relationships with people you otherwise might not know. Comment on the games shared from the games your friends play and give them tips (or a +1) if you can. Also, give them encouragement, or maybe challenge them a little to create a competitive spirit!

✔ **Be careful with whom and when you share a Games post.** From each Google+ Games post you can click the share link to share that post with your friends. This always goes to your main stream on Google+. Sharing games posts is a great way to share your friends' accomplishments with others, or share your own accomplishments with your friends, and encourage others to do better. Google+ Games are a sore spot for some on Google+, though. Some people either may not like or may not have time to play games. When you share a game to people on Google+, just try to be sure you're not polluting their stream with stuff they're not interested in. At the time of this writing, there are no filters on Google+, which makes it even more difficult to hide such posts from individuals' streams. Just keep a considerate eye out for people who may not want to see your game shares in their streams or notifications.

> ✔ **A +1 is like a "high five!"** Believe it or not, people actually do check to see who has +1d their posts on Google+. Games are no exception. Therefore, if you want to give people a "way to go!" or "keep up the good work!" just +1 their post. Many will notice and that builds relationships even further.

Challenging Your Friends

Within games, you can challenge your friends and circles to play (likely the ability to invite people to a specific game will be in a different spot in every game, although typically it's fairly evident because they want more players). In the game, you can share things like your score and then entice the friends you invite to do better (see Figure 6-4). This is a great way to nudge friends to see whether they can do better than you. After you invite your friends to play, when your friends go to their Notifications page they'll see your invitation right in their notifications stream (refer to Figure 6-3).

Using the popular Angry Birds as an example, here's how you would challenge your friends:

1. **Play the game and complete a level.**

2. **Click the leaderboard icon under your list of friends and their ranking.**

   You're taken to the leaderboard page.

3. **Click the "Invite Friends" button.**

   A dialog box that looks like Figure 6-4 appears.

4. **Choose the friends you want to invite.**

5. **Click "Preview."**

   You'll see the invite as it will appear to your friends.

6. **Make sure that's okay and hit Send to place it in your friends' notifications stream.**

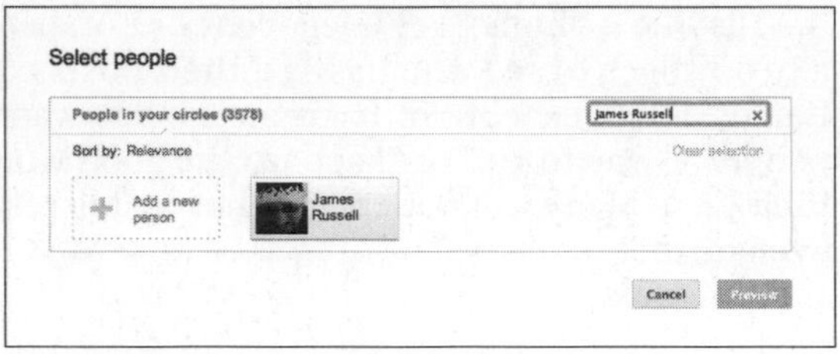

Figure 6-4: Inviting your friends or circles to play a game in Google+.

Chapter 7

Abiding by Social Network Etiquette

In This Chapter

▶ Understanding the right things to say — and *not* to say

▶ Knowing the right things to do on Google+

*O*ne of the most common worries people have on social networks (and perhaps a common critique as well) is that they're "doing it wrong." For some reason, there's always someone out there ready to critique what you're doing and, just like in real life, you do have to be careful about what you say.

In this chapter, I show you some tips that you can use on Google+ to earn the respect of your peers and those who have circled you. Google+ is still a very new network, but even on a new network you need to show respect and care for how you treat others on the network. The principles in this chapter could really apply to any social network. Keep these in mind as you post on the web.

Note: The advice in this chapter is certainly not the only way of using Google+. These are just my opinions, and I am not the Google+ police! Please use good judgment, and feel free to share with me your opinions on etiquette inside Google+ (you can circle or contact me at `http://profiles.google.com/jessestay`)! There is no single right way to use the service.

Deciding What to Post

After you know how to post on Google+, the first question on your mind may be, "What do I post?" But before you post, there's another matter to consider: finding *appropriate* things to share. Before posting, here are some questions to ask:

- ✔ **What types of content will your audience expect from you?** If the audience you're posting to is comprised primarily of PC lovers and you post good things about Macs, you may receive comments from people about how much they prefer PCs to Macs and how wrong your post is. Be very careful what you post and who you post it to — you'll get a different reaction from each type of audience.

   Refer to Chapter 3 for some tips about how to post to increase the number of circles you're in.

- ✔ **What types of things might drive your audience away?** Think about what might offend. Keep in mind that writing a slightly controversial post isn't always a bad thing — sometimes a little controversy can add to the conversation and create more comments. However, if the majority of the audience is going to turn against you because of something you post, you might want to reconsider posting it to that audience.

- ✔ **Could what you are about to post hurt you down the road in a job interview or if your mom ever saw it?** Keep in mind that anything on Google+ can be shared with a larger audience if those who have circled you choose to share it. Also, screenshots and other means of sharing can potentially incriminate you down the road.

   It's probably a good idea to leave off the drunken party pictures or posts that might embarrass you someday. Employers are increasingly relying on social networks to learn about people during the interview process. If you don't want someone to find what you shared, maybe you don't want to post it in the first place!

- ✔ **Does what you post build up or tear down others?** I always consider this question when I post. In the end, you're trying to boost the perception others have of you. Does your post strengthen or weaken the person or brand you're talking about? Are you trying to make people look better or worse? Are you trying to help others, or make it harder for them? These are all things to consider as you post on Google+.

I've noticed that when people build up other people and other brands in the posts they share, they wind up with a more positive perception of themselves. When I was young, my father always taught me the Golden Rule: "Do unto others as you would have them do unto you," and I think it applies just as much to social networks like Google+ as it does in everyday life.

Guidelines for posting

Once you've considered the preceding questions, you'll have a good idea about the approach to take when you post. The following suggestions can help guide you as you develop a strategy for posting to Google+:

✔ **Keep your posts professional.** Of course, *professionalism* is a relative term and applies essentially to the nature and purpose for your posts. For example, if you're a comedian, you'll probably want them to be funny. If you're all about business, your posts will likely be more business-oriented. On the other hand, if you're using them to update family and friends, your posts will be more personal.

✔ **This is your stage.** By this, I don't mean that your persona on Google+ should be superficial. However, you can consider Google+ as a stage, and each post you make should reflect how you want others to perceive you.

✔ **If you're not offending someone some time, "you're doing it wrong."** This is the hardest thing to embrace, and it's most applicable to people who really want to increase their audience. However, if you want your audience to grow, you'll have to accept that you'll offend a few people. Just brush it off and keep going. No need to argue or prove a point. Just politely suggest they uncircle you if they don't like what you're saying and move on.

✓ **Don't be too anxious about being uncircled.** It's okay if people do so — you just weren't for them, which really isn't a problem. You can look at being uncircled as feedback on ways to improve how you're posting to Google+. If the person uncircling you doesn't fit with your style or the persona you want to be present, just ignore the uncircle.

Overall, when developing a strategy for posting to Google+, keep a positive perspective so others will always perceive you as a positive person. Again, there's that persona thing. People will perceive you the way you present yourself. Stay positive and people will generally like you. If you're negative, they generally won't.

Commenting on others' posts

As a general rule, the suggestions in the preceding section apply to the every type of thing you post on Google+. At this point, I want to suggest a few thoughts on commenting on others' posts and status updates.

✓ **Find ways to help the person whose post you're commenting on stay positive!** I love it when people offer to help or compliment me in the posts I share. I usually don't post to get criticized by others. I always remember people who are positive and complimentary in my threads, and they are always the people I end up circling down the road. You can take the same strategy.

✓ **Keep the conversation going with others commenting, but** *don't feed the trolls.* I also love it when others continue a conversation I started. Respond to others in the thread and offer your input and opinion. However, occasionally people use sites like Google+ just to constantly disagree and tear down the people who are sharing. You generally want to avoid those people, and if they persist, just ignore them. I like it when my commenters defend me, but if a troll is just never going to give up, it's best just not to keep feeding the person.

✓ **Don't hijack the thread.** Hijacking the thread means you change the topic of the original post. If you have something unrelated to say, do so offline rather than in the thread. Hijacking the thread distracts from the conversation and can cause the conversation to go places that the original poster never intended it to go.

Knowing When to Tag Other People

Tagging, or mentioning others on Google+, can be a great way to get someone else's attention and bring that person into a conversation (see Figure 7-1). Keep in mind, however, that some people are already getting a lot of notifications, and your tag may be just one more notification that they must respond to. After many of their friends are doing this, tagging can become annoying if there is no purpose behind the tag.

To learn more about how to tag or mention your friends, check out Chapter 3.

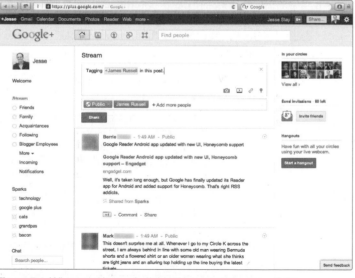

Figure 7-1: When tagging an individual in a post, do so tactfully.

Here are some general thoughts regarding tagging others on Google+:

✔ **Is the item in which you're tagging them actually related to them or something they're really interested in?** If a person likes Android and you're tagging them in an article related to the iPhone, they're really not going to be interested in your tag. Think about things individuals are truly interested in and items they may want to discuss.

✔ **Don't tag just to tag.** This is important. Just tagging people to get their attention is spam, plain and simple. Tagging them for no reason other than to get their attention is just the same as sending them an e-mail with that item you are sharing, because each post or comment you tag an individual sends them a notification (and some times even goes to their e-mail account). They are likely to respond negatively or block you as a result.

✔ **Avoid excessive tagging.** If this sounds a lot like the previous bullet, it should — it's *that* critical. If you tag people too often (even if it's something you think they'll like), they are likely to notice, uncircle you, or even block you. Keep in mind that some people have their notifications sent to their e-mail inbox, so every post you tag them in is filling their inbox. Only tag others on occasion, and only when it truly makes sense to do so.

✔ **If you don't know the person, think twice before tagging them unless you're tagging something he or she is really involved with.** If you don't know a person you're tagging and that person doesn't know you, he or she may wonder why you're tagging in the first place.

A good rule of thumb is to tag other people only when they're in an article, a post, or an image in which you're tagging them. Then you can tag them to let them know about it. If they're not in the item you're tagging them in, it's usually considered polite not to tag them.

E-mailing Others and Knowing When You Should

One nice feature of Google+ is the ability to e-mail other people from their Google+ profile — that is, if they set up the ability to contact them in their profile allowing you to do so. Assuming that's the case, follow these steps to e-mail someone else (see Figure 7-2):

1. **Go to the profile of the person you want to e-mail.**

2. **Click the Send an Email link at the left side of their profile.**

3. **In the Subject box, type the subject of your e-mail and then type your message, as you normally do in e-mails.**

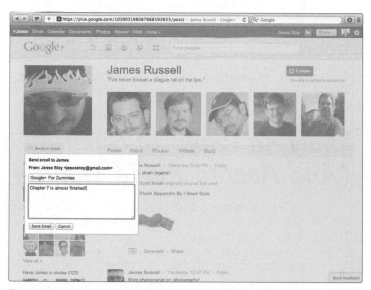

Figure 7-2: E-mailing someone through their Google+ profile.

The great thing is that no one ever has to know your e-mail address. They can send you an e-mail without you revealing too much about yourself. However, you do want to be respectful when sending someone an e-mail from their Google+ profile. Follow these tips, and you'll be fine:

✔ **Don't spam!** If you have something to sell, save that for when you know them better. Instead, spend time finding ways you can help them and compliment them in their comments. Then, when the time is right, you'll have the opportunity to tell them about what you do. Don't fill their inbox with unneeded sales pitches.

✔ **Consider whether they know you.** If they don't know you, introduce yourself and tell them why you are e-mailing them. If they've met you before, maybe a quick reminder about how they know you will help refresh their memory. (Again, don't spam them!)

✔ **Always seek to add value.** In every communication you make with others, whether you know them or not, find ways to add value from *their* perspective. How can you help them? How can you build up what they do? What are their needs?

If you follow these general tips, you'll always start off on the right foot in your communications with that individual.

Knowing When to Back Away (And How to Avoid Trolling)

As I discussed in Chapter 3, one of the worst things you can do on Google+ is to troll others. It's okay to disagree with others. It's okay to even criticize others on Google+. However, your criticisms or disagreements that aren't constructive can be quickly perceived as trolling. If you can't be convinced otherwise, it's often best to keep your disagreements to yourself.

So how can you avoid trolling? Here are some suggestions:

✔ **If you criticize, keep it constructive.** A little criticism can be good. It helps us all grow. However, if you're criticizing just to be mean or just to criticize, it can quickly become trolling. Instead, find ways to include *why* you're criticizing. How can you help the individual you're criticizing grow from what you're saying? Keep in mind that no one likes to be told they're doing something wrong just for the sake of being told they're wrong.

✔ **If you disagree, be open to being convinced you could be wrong.** *Never* ignore the possibility that you could be the one who is wrong. Often the person doing the posting has put a lot of thought into the post. You could very likely be wrong. Look long and hard at what the person doing the posting is saying. If you are wrong, accept the fact that they were right and you were wrong. No one is perfect, and sometimes admitting that fact is the best way to build relationships.

✔ **Agree to disagree.** Even if you're not wrong, let it go. If you still disagree, don't continue the disagreement and be willing to give up your criticism after you've made your point. If you can't come to an agreement, state your disagreement once and let it be. There's no sense continuing to argue — you made your point. Continuing an argument with someone who wasn't intending to argue in the first place is a good way to get blocked from a conversation. There's no sense continuing to tear down the individual who is posting.

If you avoid trolling, you are far less likely to be uncircled or blocked, and you'll build much stronger relationships in the end. Most of all, do what makes sense! Treat others as you would have them treat you.

Chapter 8

Using Google+ on Mobile Devices

* *

In This Chapter
▶ Using the Google+ app on iOS and Android devices
▶ Using Google+ on a mobile web browser

* *

*T*he smartphone experience is quickly overtaking desktop experiences as the number one way to access the web around the world. It makes sense therefore that Google would make Google+ apps for mobile devices a priority (and now that Google has bought Motorola, it makes even *more* sense). If you have a mobile device, there's a good chance you'll want to use Google+ on that device.

In this chapter I show you the different device options for Google+ and how you can access Google+ on each device. I also talk about huddles and ways you can make the most of your phone's features to share with your friends on Google+.

Understanding the Google+ Mobile App Experience

As I write this, Google+ is available for two different mobile operating systems and the mobile web. On both Android and iOS phones and tablet devices there is an official app you can download to use Google+ on your device. On other devices with a web browser you can access plus.google.com and still get the Google+ experience. I'll show you the details of each in the following section.

Using Google+ on an iOS or Android device

As I mentioned, Google has, at least at the time of this writing, created apps for two basic mobile devices, which I'll refer to as "experiences" — the Android experience and the iOS (iPhone, iPod Touch, and iPad) experience. On the surface, the experience of using the Google+ app on these two devices is virtually identical. However, because of limitations in the iOS operating system, the iOS experience is not nearly as deeply integrated into the operating system as the Android experience.

For this reason I'll refer to the iOS experience as the Google+ *mobile basic experience*. This experience exists across both iOS and Android devices (see Figure 8-1). I cover what Android (owned by Google) adds to this experience in the next section.

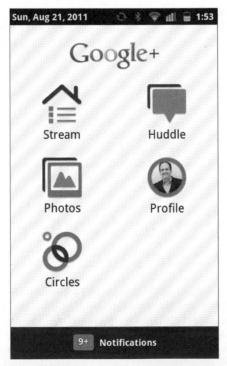

Figure 8-1: The basic Google+ experience for mobile devices starts here.

In the mobile basic experience on Google+, you can do the following:

- ✔ Post updates

- ✔ Comment on posts

- ✔ View your circled friends' updates

- ✔ Target your updates to specific circles

- ✔ Post and view photos

- ✔ View your notifications

In addition, the following list shows there are some unique features of Google+ that you can make use of only on a mobile device (they aren't available on the desktop). Although I cover these features in detail in the last few sections of this chapter, starting with the "Checking in" section. Here's a preview:

- ✔ Check in with your current location.

- ✔ See the posts of people who are near where you are at any given time.

- ✔ Participate in huddles or group chats with other Google+ users.

Using Google+ features only on Android devices

In addition to the features mentioned in the preceding section, Android provides a few other basic features that integrate well with the Android operating system, including the following:

- ✔ **Automatic detection of your Google credentials:** As with many apps on Android, Google+ uses Android's built-in Intents API. This special feature of Android allows your device to automatically detect whether you've registered your Google account with your device. If so, you can just use your already stored Google Account to log on to Google+, which enables you to immediately start using Google+ and share with friends!

✔ **Sharing from any app on your device:** This feature is also part of the Intents API. Google+ enables any app on your device to add Google+ as one of the sharing options on your device. For example, if you take a picture on your device and the Google+ app is installed, you'll see Google+ as one of the options to share photos (see Figure 8-2). Just select the option to share a photo you took on your phone with Google+ and your photo, if you've registered your Google account with your device, immediately goes straight to Google+! This process works for any application that utilizes this feature.

Figure 8-2: Sharing photos through the Share option on Android.

✔ **Google+ widget:** When you install Google+, you'll see a new widget on your device (see Figure 8-3). From your lists of widgets you can install the Google+ widget to your Android desktop and immediately start sharing to Google+ without ever needing to open the app.

Google + Widget

Figure 8-3: The Google+ widget on my Nexus 3 (near top of screen).

🖊 **Integration with your device's settings button:** With Google+ open, you can tap your Android device's settings button and settings for the Google+ app will appear (see Figure 8-4). On this screen, you can send feedback to the Google+ team, set your notification preferences, and toggle your instant upload settings (see the next bullet).

If you ever have an issue with the Google+ app on your phone, be sure to submit feedback to the Google+ team! This unique feature allows Google to improve the experience and identify flaws in the app. Google actually wants you to tell them what they can do better!

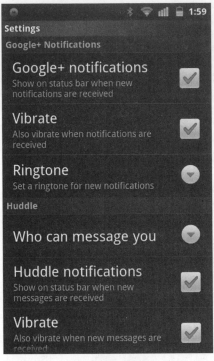

Figure 8-4: Your Google+ settings on Android.

✔ **Instant upload of photos and videos:** One convenient feature of the Android Google+ app is the ability to instantly upload photos and videos to a private web album. You'll be prompted to turn this on the first time you open the Google+ app on Android, or you can go into your settings and turn it on there by just checking the box next to Instant Upload (see Figure 8-5).

These photos and videos will remain archived and private until you decide whom to share them with on Google+.

Instant Upload can be a great way to keep backups of every picture or video you take on your phone. It also means you don't have to spend time uploading them later!

Figure 8-5: Turning on Instant Upload in your Google+ settings on Android.

Using Google+ on the mobile web

If you don't use an iOS or Android device, or you prefer not to use their apps, Google does provide a high-quality *mobile web experience* (which, again, is my term for using Google+ via a phone's web browser). To see what that experience looks like, see Figure 8-6. To get to the mobile web experience, just go to http://plus.google.com on your mobile device.

The Google+ experience on your mobile web browser is similar to what you would have in a desktop experience, but in a much more condensed and easy-to-consume format that is built for a smaller device. With the exception of huddles, you get the basic mobile experience mentioned in the "Using Google+ on an iOS or Android device" section earlier in the chapter.

Figure 8-6: The Google+ mobile web experience.

Posting to Google+ on a Mobile Device

As you open your preferred experience on your mobile device, you'll see that the experience is very similar to the desktop experience I talk about throughout this book. Here are some basic steps to begin posting on your mobile device:

1. **Open the Google+ app in the list of apps on your phone or surf with your phone's browser at** http:// plus.google.com.

With the exception of the mobile web experience, you'll be greeted with a splash screen where you can choose what to do (refer to Figure 8-1).

2. **On the splash screen, tap the Stream icon to begin viewing your stream and posting.**

   If you're on the mobile web experience, you're already on the stream.

3. **To begin posting to your stream, tap the pencil icon on your device (see Figure 8-7).**

   A screen like the one shown in Figure 8-8 appears. This "All circles" stream screen should appear similarly on all devices.

Figure 8-7: Tap the pencil icon to begin posting on your mobile device.

Figure 8-8: The basic posting screen on Google+ mobile apps (may vary slightly by device).

4. **Type your status update and add your location if you want to.**

5. **Choose the circles you want to post to (it defaults to Public) and add a photo if necessary.**

6. **Tap Post.**

   Your post goes live immediately.

Uploading photos on a mobile device

There are multiple ways to upload photos to your device. On the mobile web experience, at least at this writing, you can't upload photos. However, on the Android and iOS apps for Google+, you can.

If you're on an Android device, you can select the option to automatically upload your photos to Google+. You can then share those from your private album, if you like. I talk more about this in Chapter 9.

On Android, you can opt to share your photos straight from the photo app on your phone. On both types of devices, you can also attach a photo to a status update, as mentioned in the previous section.

Or, by tapping the little camera or photo icon in the Android widget, it will take you straight to either the camera view or to pick from your photo albums on your phone, respectively. This can be a quick way to share to Google+ in as few steps as possible.

On iOS and Android devices, the final way to share photos on Google+ is to click Photos on the splash screen:

1. **Open the Google+ app on your phone and tap the Photos icon on the splash page that appears.**

2. **Tap the camera icon (see Figure 8-9).**

3. **Choose Take Photo to take a photo from your camera or choose Select Photo to select one from your phone's albums.**

4. **If you chose Select Photo, a screen will appear with your phone's photo albums. Check the box next to all the photos you want to share and select Share. If you chose Take Photo, a camera view for your phone will appear. Just take your picture.**

On iOS devices, the Take Photo and Select Photo buttons are two separate buttons, very similar to the buttons in the Android widget. To take a photo, tap the camera button. To select a photo, tap the little button next to it that looks like two photographs stacked on top of each other.

5. **Type a message to go with your photos.**

6. **Select the circles you want to share to.**

7. **Select a location (if you choose).**

8. **Tap Post to post your photos.**

Figure 8-9: Choose one of two options to select a photo to share.

Checking in

Checking in on Google+ is a great way to share with your friends where you are and what you're doing. With each *check in,* a map of the location is shared (that links to Google Maps so you can see where it is in bigger context) along with your post. Checking in is simple. To check in on Google+, follow these steps:

1. **Open the Google+ app and tap the Stream icon on the splash page that appears.**

   You can skip this step on the mobile web experience.

2. **Tap the check box icon in the upper right corner.**

   Google+ automatically lists a few places based on your GPS location.

3. **Choose a location, or search for another one and select one.**

   This step takes you back to the posting page.

4. **Enter a post to add to your location.**

5. **Attach any relevant photos by following the steps outlined in the previous section.**

6. **Select the circles you want to post to by tapping on the input field at the top with the arrow pointing right and typing in the name of the circle or circles you choose (refer to Figure 8-8).**

   You're done!

Viewing the "Nearby" Stream

Another unique feature of the mobile app for Google+ is the *nearby stream*. The nearby stream is a stream of updates from people closest to your current location on Google+. This feature can provide a great way to find Google+ users who live near you or are participating near your current location.

To access the nearby stream, do the following:

1. **Open the mobile web in a web browser or tap Stream from your splash page in the app.**

2. **Swipe to the right and you're taken to the Nearby stream.**

 On Android devices (and likely iOS devices soon after this book goes to print), you can also reshare any post you see in your stream just as you can on the web. To reshare a post on your Android device, just tap the post you'd like to reshare. On the resulting screen for that post, tap the "..." button in the upper right and then tap Share This Post in the drop-down menu.

Using Huddles to Chat with Groups

Huddles are a unique feature to the mobile apps (they aren't available on the mobile web). They allow you to chat with groups of people you specify, or with groups you are invited to. To use huddles, follow these steps:

1. **Open the app and tap the Huddle icon on the splash page that appears.**

   The list of huddles you've been invited to appears, if there are any as yet (see Figure 8-10).

Figure 8-10: Your list of huddles in Google+.

2. To join a huddle, just tap one and then tap Let's Huddle; to opt out instead, just tap No Thanks.

3. To start your own huddle, tap the little Huddle icon in the upper right corner of the Huddles page.

4. Type the names, e-mail addresses, or circles of other Google+ users.

5. Add a message to start the huddle.

   You've started your first huddle!

Chapter 9

Using Google+ Photos

In This Chapter

▶ Viewing your own photos and those from your circles

▶ Setting privacy for your photos

▶ Posting photos to your profile

*A*long with Google+ comes one of the most social photo-sharing experiences available. Google+ provides an entire photo library built into the experience that allows users to upload, store, and share photos. Google+ photos are integrated into every element of the Google+ experience, allowing you to share those "Kodak moments" as they happen throughout your life.

In this chapter, I show you how to use Google+ photos, including the features that are available to you and what you can do with them. I show you how to keep your photos private, if you choose to, and how you can discover new photos from your circles.

Viewing Your Photos

First things first. To get to your photos page, just click the Photos icon at the top of Google+ (indicated by the arrow in Figure 9-1). The photos page appears showing photos of all the people you've circled. On the left are links of the types of photos you can view and on the right are photos you've taken and uploaded, as well as a button to upload more photos and below that a list of images from your phone or albums on Google+.

Photos button

Figure 9-1: You can access the photos page in Google+ via the Photos icon.

You can review your own photos three ways:

- ✔ Photos taken of you, or photos you were tagged in
- ✔ Photos taken on your Android phone that were uploaded automatically
- ✔ Photos you've uploaded

Viewing photos taken of you

The Photos of You link includes photos you've been tagged in by your friends. Ideally, these will be photos with you in them, but as you can see from mine (see Figure 9-2) you do not actually have to be in the photo for people to tag you as being in the photo. You can, of course, change who can tag you in photos by editing your profile settings. I show you how to edit those settings in Chapter 1.

Figure 9-2: My Photos of You page.

To view photos taken of you, just click the Photos of You link in the left column of the photos page and click the photos to see larger versions of each.

You can navigate through each photo by pressing the right and left arrows on your keyboard.

Viewing photos taken on your phone

As I mention in Chapter 8, on an Android phone you can choose to automatically upload your photos and videos to Google+. (This feature is available only on Android, unfortunately.) By clicking the Photos from Your Phone link on the left, you can view these one by one (see Figure 9-3).

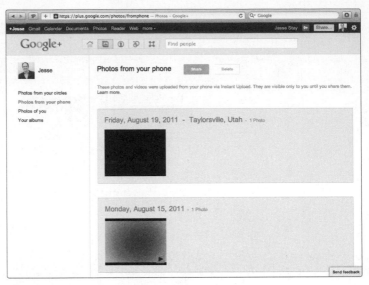

Figure 9-3: The Photos from Your Phone page.

Google+ shows the option as Photos, but it really means Photos and Videos. If you've taken videos on your Android phone and enabled it to automatically upload photos and videos to Google+, you'll see that the videos will appear as well. When you click the Upload Photos button, which I cover in the section "Uploading New Photos" later in the chapter, you can also upload videos with that button.

Viewing photos you've uploaded

To view photos or videos you've uploaded, just click Your Albums in the left column of your photos page (see Figure 9-4).

Photo and videos you've uploaded (other than the automatically uploaded photos and videos from your Android phone) will appear here. Notice that they're sorted into albums. You may see a few default albums:

✔ **Photos from posts:** As you post with photos, as I show in Chapter 8, each photo you upload with a post is stored in this album. As a result, you can always go back and reference your previously posted photos if you like.

✔ **Profile photos:** Any time you change your profile picture, the new picture is stored in this album. You can go to this page to find an archive of all the profile pictures you've uploaded in the past.

✔ **Photos from Blogger.com blogs (separated as albums by blog):** If you have a blog on Blogger.com, any time you upload a photo or picture to your blog it will appear in this album. If you have multiple Blogger.com blogs, each blog will be represented by a different album, organized by the name of your blog.

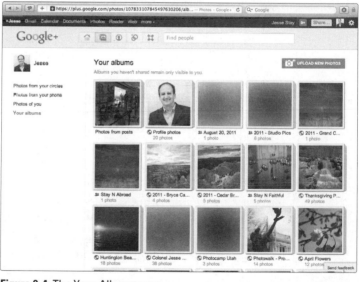

Figure 9-4: The Your Albums page.

Viewing Photos from Your Circles

A fun and easy way to browse Google+ is by viewing the pictures your friends have uploaded. You can do so simply by going to the default photos page or by clicking the Photos from Your Circles link in the left column of the photos page. Similarly to the photo views from the "Viewing Your Photos" section earlier in the chapter, you'll notice several things about each photo you click from your circles (see Figure 9-5):

- ✔ **The photo:** The photo is usually a pretty good resolution. This characteristic makes it an ideal environment for photographers wanting to share their photos with friends and clients.

- ✔ **Actions:** If you click Actions, a drop-down list will appear where you'll see options like Photo Details and Report Abuse. You can report the photo via this means. Or if you click Photo Details, you can get detailed information that the camera stored about the photo (if it's available – some cameras do not store this information) — things such as exposure, aperture, shutter speed, camera type, and even location are exposed here!

- ✔ **Tagging:** You can tag other friends using this button. (I cover this in the "Tagging Others in Photos" section later in the chapter.)

- ✔ **Next and previous photos:** These are all the photos in sequence. You can also use your arrow keys to navigate.

- ✔ **Comments for the photo:** In the right column you can comment on each photo or picture.

Commenting on photos is easy! Just click the photo you want to comment on and click in the box that says Add a Comment.

Figure 9-5: The individual photo view in Google+.

Uploading New Photos

You're probably excited to start uploading some photos. There are so many ways to upload a photo on Google+, and I've shown you several already in Chapter 8. For this chapter I'm going to stick to just the photos page in Google+ and how you can upload photos there. To upload a new photo or video (see Figure 9-6), follow these steps:

1. **Click the Photos button on your main Google+ page.**

   Your Photos page appears.

2. **Click the Upload New Photos button in the upper right corner of the photos page.**

   A pop-up dialog box appears, prompting you to start uploading photos (it looks like Figure 9-6).

   3. **Click Select Photos from Your Computer.**

      You are prompted to select the files from your com-
      puter's hard drive that you would like to upload to
      Google+.

   4. **Choose the photos or videos on your hard drive you
      want to upload.**

   5. **Name your album.**

      You can do this in the text input box at the top of the
      Upload and share photos dialog box.

   6. **Click the Create Album button.**

      An album will be created with the name you selected
      and you'll be prompted to share with your circles.
      Select the circles you want to share with, add a com-
      ment, and you're done.

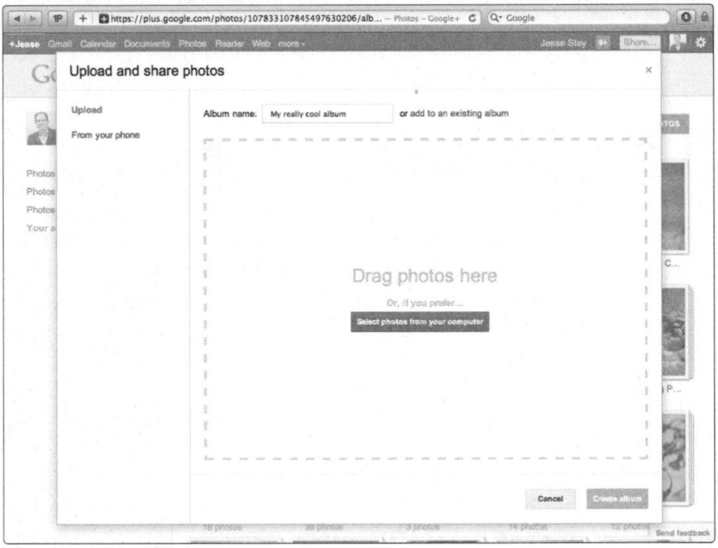

Figure 9-6: Uploading a photo or video in Google+.

Tagging Others in Photos

You can tag people in your circles on anyone's photo on Google+. When you tag an individual in any photo, that individual will be notified via their notifications. They can then remove the tag or approve it, and the photo will appear with the tag of that individual's name in it.

Be sure you follow the etiquette rules in Chapter 7. Tagging excessively can be spammy!

To tag someone, follow these steps:

1. **Click the photo you want to tag.**

2. **Click the Add Tag button (see Figure 9-7).**

3. **Expand the square around the face of the individual you're trying to tag.**

4. **Type the name of the person you want to tag and select that individual in the list provided.**

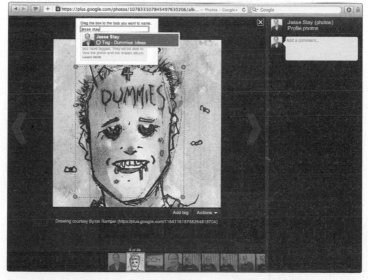

Figure 9-7: Tagging photos in Google+ via the Add Tag button.

Google+ automatically detects faces in your photos. If you hover your mouse cursor over a face in a photo, a box appears giving you the option to Click to Name. Click that option and you'll be able to tag the individual in that manner.

Configuring Privacy Settings for Your Photos

If you go to the Your Albums section of your photos page, you can set the privacy settings of your albums. To change the privacy of an album, follow these steps:

1. **Click the album.**

2. **Next to Visible to, click Edit.**

   You'll see what circles your album is visible to there (see Chapter 2 to learn more about circles) — it will likely say Everyone or Limited.

3. **In the pop-up box that appears, type individual people and circles you want that album to be visible to.**

   If you want everyone to see it, choose Public. If you also want to target another circle, choose that as well (see Figure 9-8). The point is you can choose whatever circles you want to see that photo.

   Your album will now be visible only to those you specified.

 Narrowing who can see your photos to select circles is a great way to be sure that pictures of your kids are being shared only with the people you want to see them. Or maybe your employer doesn't need to see your party pics. You can target those party pics here as well, by selecting a circle that doesn't include your employer, for example.

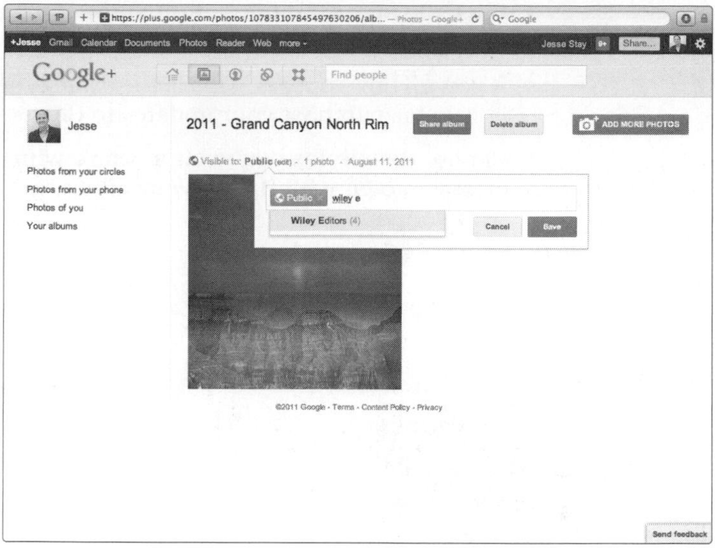

Figure 9-8: Setting privacy settings for your albums in Google+.

Sharing Your Photos

After you've uploaded a few photos you may want to share them with your friends. Of course, you can always just upload them with your posts and share them that way, but you may want to share a photo or two after the fact.

As of this writing, unless you're uploading them with your posts or through your phone, you can share entire albums only after the fact. To share an album with your friends, follow these steps:

1. **Go to Your Albums.**
2. **Click the album you want to share.**

3. **Click the Share Album button at the top (see Figure 9-9).**

   A pop-up box appears. This is the same type of dialog box you use to post your updates to Google+.

4. **Choose the circles you want to share with, enter a message to go with it, and your album will be shared with your stream.**

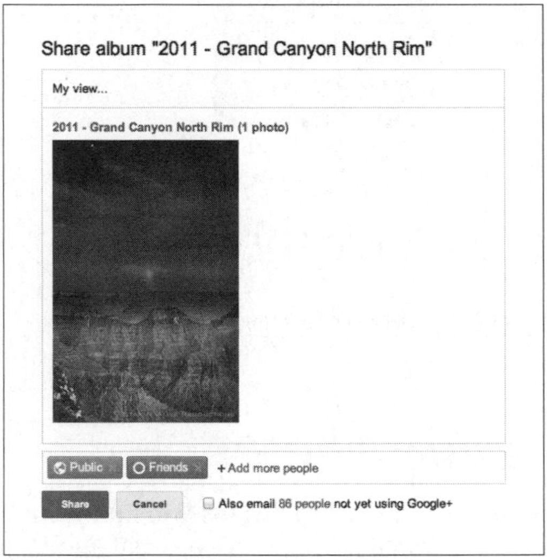

Share album "2011 - Grand Canyon North Rim"

My view...

2011 - Grand Canyon North Rim (1 photo)

Public   Friends   + Add more people

Share   Cancel   ☐ Also email 86 people not yet using Google+

Figure 9-9: Sharing albums to your stream.

Chapter 10

Liberating (Exporting and Backing Up) Your G+ Data

In This Chapter

▶ Discovering what you can back up on Google+

▶ Understanding how to back up your data on Google+

*G*oogle+ has a very flexible and very unique feature that enables you to back up everything you upload to the service. It may be that you, heaven forbid, want to cancel your Google+ account and want to be sure you have a copy of all that precious data you uploaded to the service. Google's okay with that (although likely disappointed)! Or maybe you just want to be safe and have a backup here or there.

If you care about the data you're storing on Google+, it's a good idea to make occasional backups. In this chapter I show you how to back up your data, what types of data can be backed up, and what to do with that data once you back it up.

Knowing What You Can Back Up

Google+ allows you to back up all your data or just pieces of it.

 Backing up this data is not just limited to Google+; Google pulls in elements from other Google products (such as your photos from Picasa Web or your contacts from Gmail) to allow you to back up those items as well.

Using Google+ you can back up the following to your computer's hard drive:

- ✓ **Articles that you have +1d:** Google search results, articles, and web pages on which you clicked the +1 button will be included in your download.

- ✓ **Your Google Buzz posts (if you're a Google Buzz user):** Google Buzz is a news aggregation service integrated into Gmail that you can use to read news from your friends. Google Buzz is considered a predecessor to Google+, and you can show your aggregated posts from around the web as a tab in Google+. If you choose to back up these posts, they will be downloaded.

- ✓ **All your Google contacts and circles:** This is a great way to back up your contact data.

- ✓ **All your photos (including those saved as copies on Picasa Web):** These are all the photos you've uploaded to Google+ and any you've uploaded to Picasa Web in the past as well.

    Google+ Photos is tightly integrated with Picasa Web photos. The two are, in essence, one and the same. When you upload a photo to one, the photo will appear in the other. I anticipate that Picasa Web will eventually become just Google+ Photos. See Chapter 9 for more info about Google+ Photos.

- ✓ **Your profile data:** This is all the data you've stored with your Google+ profile.

- ✓ **Your stream data:** This includes every post you've ever posted to Google+.

You can choose one of these options, some of them, or all of them, and they will be downloaded to your hard drive after you follow the steps in the next section.

Backing Up Your Data

Backing up your data is very easy on Google+. To back up everything, just follow these steps:

1. **Click the little gear icon in the upper right corner of the Google+ sandbar and click Google+ Settings in the drop-down menu that appears.**

   The Google+ Account Settings page appears.

2. **On the left, click Data Liberation.**

   The Data liberation settings page appears (see Figure 10-1).

3. **Click Download Your Data.**

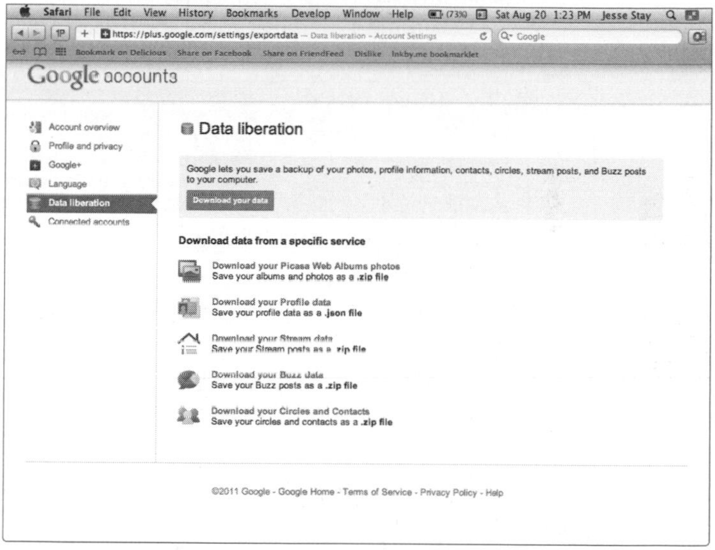

Figure 10-1: Your Data Liberation Settings page.

4. **To download everything, just click Create Archive. To download individual items from Google+, click Choose Services and you can pick which services you want to back up. You can also just click one of the individual links below the Create Archive button (see Figure 10-1).**

   You'll be taken to a really cool page with moving bars signifying that your data is being backed up (see Figure 10-2).

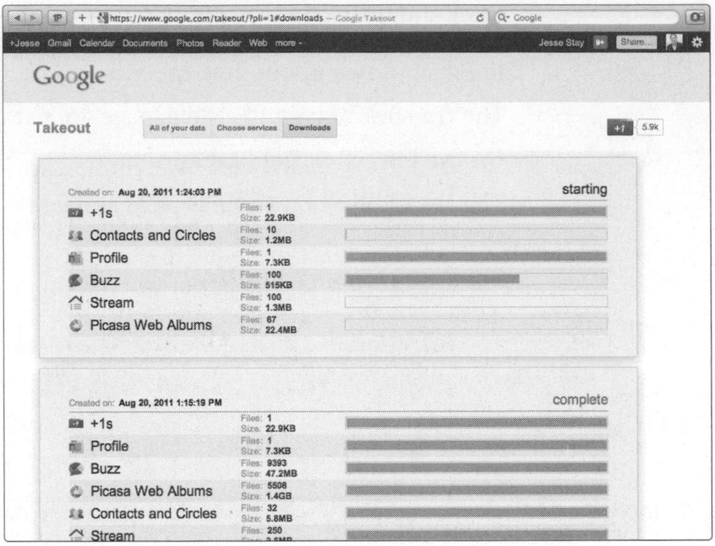

Figure 10-2: Your uber cool download page.

5. When the archive is done, click the Download button.

You may be asked to authenticate; if so, once you do as asked, the download will start.

After the file has downloaded, a zipped file will appear on your hard drive. You probably won't need to unzip it with a program like WinZip; versions of Windows since Windows XP and modern Macs handle zip files natively, so you should be able to just double-click it.

Now, all your data will be in an organized format in a folder on your hard drive, as follows:

✔ Buzz and Google+ posts will be stored in HTML files.

✔ Contacts will be in .vcf contact format that most e-mail programs can understand.

✔ Profile is stored in a simple format that other profile apps on the web can read.

✔ +1s are stored as bookmark files that you can import as bookmarks into your browser.

Exporting your contacts can be a great way to share your circles with your friends. To share a circle, just back up your contacts, as explained in this section. Each circle will show up under the Contacts folder as a separate file with a .vcf extension appended to the file. To import someone else's circle into your own, just go to your circles page on Google+, click Find People, and select Import Address Book. Select the .vcf file for the circle you want to import and voila, all your friends' people in the circle they shared with you will appear for you to add to your own circle. It's important to note however that some of the contacts you share may contain personal details such as phone numbers and addresses, so be careful who you share these circles with!

Chapter 11

Ten Third-Party Applications You Can Use Right Now

In This Chapter

▶ Using extensions for Google+

▶ Using websites for Google+

*A*s of this writing, Google has just released a formal developer Application Programming Interface (API) for building Google+ applications. Although Google has allowed a few select gaming developers to build games for its platform, not many other developers have created apps yet for Google+. By the time you read this, of course, I fully expect this to change — there may be a good chance that many of these apps will even use that new platform.

Because the Google+ developer API just barely launched to the public, until very recently developers worked around the previous lack of an application platform by building browser extensions that you can install in Google's Chrome web browser (and in some cases other browsers). In this chapter I share ten of my favorite Google+ extensions.

 Because until very recently Google+ had not previously released a programming interface for applications to be created, to create many extensions developers used a technique called *scraping,* which means to read the HTML of the Google+ site and modify the site based on that HTML. So, use caution as you try these extensions, because if Google+ ever changes its interface (and it will) and thus the HTML of the Google+ site, all of these extensions are prone to break until they implement Google's new developer API. Don't say I didn't warn you!

Klout

Klout indexes the social networks that you use and determines what areas of interest you have "Klout" in. It then produces a score that you can compare against your friends. Klout provides "perks" (real life products they mail to you) to those that have clout in given areas. Shortly before this writing Klout also added Google+ integration so that you can now measure your influence on Google+ in addition to the other services Klout offers. You can sign up for Klout at:

```
https://klout.com
```

Reader to Plus

If you're a Google Reader user like me (Google Reader is a site that allows you to subscribe to updates on other blogs and websites; try it out at `http://reader.google.com`), you may want a simple way of sharing to Google+ from Google Reader. At this writing, there is no native way to share from Google Reader to Google+. This extension makes that possible by adding a little Share to Google+ link at the bottom of each post in Google Reader. Download Reader to Plus from:

```
https://chrome.google.com/webstore/detail/
ellpglpgjfcfppiljfokjoconaheaiff
```

Press Shift+G in Google Reader to share to Google+ with this extension installed.

Extended Share for Google+

If you want to share your posts on Google+ to Facebook or Twitter or another social network, this is a great extension to

install. It adds a Share On link at the bottom of each Google+
post (next to the Share link), allowing users to share to their
favorite social networks. You can download Extended Share
for Google+ from:

```
https://chrome.google.com/webstore/detail/
oenpjldbckebacipkfbcoppmiflglnib
```

Google+ Hangout Check

This extension places an icon in your Chrome browser that
turns blue if any of your friends on Google+ are having a
hangout. Click on it and it shows each of your friends that are
hanging out currently. If you're looking for people to hang out
with, check out Google+ Hangout Check at the following site:

```
https://chrome.google.com/webstore/detail/
mbgdijeginmoajogfmogadhnfbbcflfd
```

Replies and More for Google+

Ever participate in a conversation with a lot of comments and
find it hard to figure out who you're responding to? Rather
than pressing the plus (+) key and trying to spell the name
right, you can just click Reply, which appears when you
mouse over the comment. Then the name of the individual
you're replying to automatically populates the comment box.
You can download Replies and More for Google+ from:

```
https://chrome.google.com/webstore/detail/
fgmhgfecnmeljhchgcjlfldjiepcfpea
```

Plus Minus

If your main stream is getting too noisy or is filled with users
like me who post a lot, you can use this extension to clean up
your stream a little. This extension allows you to collapse all
posts, with a little comment notification icon specifying the
number of new comments on the post. You can also specify
which circles you want to appear in your stream. You can

configure it with what you want to appear in your stream. You can download Plus Minus from:

```
https://chrome.google.com/webstore/detail/
pidkbnhjgdngcfcaikoocdanfijkgdli
```

Surplus

Surplus puts a Google+ notification on top of your Chrome browser, so no matter what website you're visiting you can see how many notifications you have. In addition, you can respond and post without ever leaving the sites you're visiting. You can download Surplus from:

```
https://chrome.google.com/webstore/detail/
pfphgaimeghgekhncbkfblhdhfaiaipf
```

+Photo Zoom

This Chrome extension makes all the pictures shared on Google+ show up bigger when you mouse over them. You can use it as a shortcut to seeing full-sized images rather than having to click them. You can download +Photo Zoom from:

```
https://chrome.google.com/webstore/detail/
njoglkofocgopmdfjnbifnicbickbola
```

SocialStatistics.com

SocialStatistics.com is a website (not a browser extension) that shows you how people rank in Google+. You can find out which users are being circled the most and where you rank on Google+ in that regard. Visit this website at:

```
http://socialstatistics.com/
```

Be careful measuring your success based on rankings for SocialStatistics.com; the site only tracks those users who add their names to their list manually and are therefore only tracking a small sampling of Google+ users at the time of this writing.

G+ Stream Pause

Is your Google+ stream moving too fast for you? As I write this, if my stream updates while I am writing a comment my comment will gradually move down the page as I'm typing. This can get quite annoying! The Google+ Stream Pause Chrome extension allows you to pause your stream. Any new updates that occur while it is paused will appear in a counter at the top of your stream and will not update until you un-pause the stream. Download Google+ Stream Pause from:

```
https://chrome.google.com/webstore/detail/
clelpdcobdkbcjfcfcmkoeldfobapohe
```

Go for More!

Looking for more apps or extensions to try out for Google+? There's a great website at `http://googleplusapps.tumblr.com` that you can subscribe to in your favorite RSS reader (such as `http://reader.google.com`). The site shares newly found apps and provides a review of each. It's a great resource for people passionate about Google+, like me!

Index

• Numerics •

+1 buttons, 17, 18–19, 44

• A •

About page, filling out, 11–14
accounts, creating, 5–8
Android devices, 90–95
applications
  Extended Share, 124–125
  G+ Stream Pause, 127
  Google+ Hangout Check, 125
  Klout website, 124
  overview, 123
  Plus Minus, 125–126
  +Photo Zoom, 126
  Reader to Plus, 124
  Replies and More, 125
  searching for, 127
  SocialStatistics website, 126
  Surplus, 126

• B •

backing up data, 117–121
beta, closed, 36
beta, open, 36
blocking trolls, 60–61
Blogger.com blogs, 109
Buzz, Google, 17, 118

• C •

challenging friends at gaming,
  77–78
circles
  adding people to, 32–33
  consuming content for, 33–36

creating, 29–32
importance of profile for, 9
inviting people to Google+, 36–38
organizing followers on, 20
overview, 27
posting options for, 23–24
posting to, 48–49
profile privacy, 38–41
settings for, 14–16
understanding, 27–28
using Home section on About
  page for, 13
viewing photos from, 110–111
comments
  criticism in, 87
  deleting, 55–56
  disabling, 56–57
  getting people to write, 53
  mentioning others in, 53
  on photos, 110
  social network etiquette for,
    82–83
contacts, importing, 20
controversial posts, 80

• D •

data, exporting and backing up,
  117–121
deleting
  comments, 55–56
  posts, 55
destination of posts, 23–24
disabling comments or reshares,
  56–57
Drop Here to Create a New Circle
  circle, 29–30, 31

• *E* •

editing posts, 54–55
e-mail, 50, 85–86
etiquette
  avoiding trolling, 86–87
  e-mailing, 85–86
  overview, 79
  posts, 80–83
  tagging people, 83–84
exporting data, 117–121
Extended Share application, 124–125

• *F* •

family, sharing posts with, 44–45
following
  organizing followers, 20
  overview, 19
  picking people for, 19–20
friends
  challenging at gaming, 77–78
  notifying about posts, 25
  sharing posts with, 44–45

• *G* •

G+ Stream Pause application, 127
gaming
  challenging friends, 77–78
  finding games, 73–76
  overview, 73
  reading games stream, 76–77
geo location option, turning off, 16
Google account
  creating, 7
  signing in with, 6–7
Google Buzz, 17, 118
Google+ Hangout Check
  application, 125
Google+ profile. *See* profiles
Google+ widget, 92–93
graphics, sharing, 23, 51, 52
groups, communicating with, 46

• *H* •

hangouts, 63–67
hijacking the thread, 82–83
huddles feature, 102–103

• *I* •

ignoring trolls, 58–59
images. *See* photos
importing contacts, 20
Incoming link, 35
individuals, posting to, 49–50
Intents API, Android, 91–92
invitations
  accepting, 5–6
  to games, 75
  inviting to Google+, 36–38
iOS devices, 90–91

• *K* •

Kawasaki, Guy, 47
keyboard shortcuts, 25
Klout website, 124

• *L* •

life journals, 46
links, sharing, 23
location, sharing, 23

• *M* •

messages, choosing, 22–23
mobile basic experience, 90–91
mobile devices
  Android devices, 90–95
  huddles feature, 102–103
  iOS devices, 90–91
  mobile web, 95–96
  nearby stream feature, 101

overview, 89–126
posting on, 96–101
mobile web experience, 95–96
moderating posts
  deleting comments, 55–56
  deleting posts, 55
  disabling comments or reshares,
    56–57
  editing, 54–55
  muting posts, 55
  overview, 54
monitoring posts, 50
muting
  others in hangout, 66
  posts, 55

• *N* •

names, using real, 8
nearby stream feature, 101
notification bubble, 22
notifications
  about circles, 25
  of games, 75
Notifications link, 35, 36

• *P* •

personal updates, 45
phones, photos taken on, 107–108
photos. *See also* viewing photos
  backing up, 118
  Edit mode, options in, 16
  invisibility option for, 16
  mobile devices, uploading from,
    98–100
  overview, 105
  privacy settings, 16, 114–115
  in scrapbook section of profile, 10
  setting profile, 8
  sharing, 51, 52, 115–116

tagging others in, 113–114
uploading, 94, 98–100, 111–112
Plus Minus application, 125–126
+1 buttons, 17, 18–19, 44
+Photo Zoom application, 126
poll question posts, 57
posts
  about games, 76–77
  circles, posting to, 48–49
  circling people, increasing
    number of, 47–48
  destination of, choosing, 23–24
  e-mail addresses, posting to, 50
  getting people to comment on, 53
  groups, communicating with
    specific, 46
  individuals, posting to, 49–50
  life journals, 46
  mentioning others in, 53
  message, choosing, 22–23
  mobile devices, posting on,
    96–101
  moderating, 54–57
  monitoring, 50
  notifying friends, 25
  overview, 22, 43
  +1's for, 18
  resharing, 51–53, 56–57
  sharing only with friends and
    family, 44–45
  social network etiquette for,
    80–83
  trolls, 57–61
privacy settings, 16–18, 38–41,
  114–115
professional posts, 81
profiles
  circle settings, 14–16
  creating, 8
  filling out About page, 11–14
  overview, 11
  privacy options, 16–18, 38–41

• R •

Reader to Plus application, 124
reading games stream, 76–77
reading with sparks, 71–72
Replies and More application, 125
resharing posts, 51–53, 56–57

• S •

sandbar, 18, 21–22
scraping, 123
settings
  circle, 14–16
  overall privacy, 16–18
  photo privacy, 16–17, 114–115
  profile privacy, 38–41
sharing
  graphics, 23, 51, 52
  links, 23
  photos, 115–116
  posts only with friends and
    family, 44–45
  resharing posts, 51–53, 56–57
  sparks, 72
social network etiquette
  avoiding trolling, 86–87
  e-mailing, 85–86
  overview, 79
  posts, 80–83
  tagging people, 83–84
SocialStatistics website, 126
sparks feature
  overview, 69
  picking, 69–71
  reading and interacting with,
    71–72
Surplus application, 126

• T •

tagging people, 47–48, 83–84,
  113–114

tags, photo, 16
text chat, 66
trolls
  avoiding trolling, 86–87
  blocking, 60–61
  handling, 57–58
  ignoring, 58–59
  overview, 57

• U •

uploading photos
  with Android Google+ app, 94
  from mobile devices, 98–100
  on Photos page, 111–112

• V •

video
  from phone, viewing, 107–108
  sharing, 23
  tips for hangout, 64
  privacy settings, 16
  uploading, 94, 111–112
  viewing uploaded, 108–109
Videos tab, 16
viewing photos
  from circles, 110–111
  overview, 105–106
  taken by others, 106–107
  taken on phones, 107–108
  uploaded, 108–109

• W •

widget, Google+, 92–93

• Y •

YouTube video, watching over
  hangout, 66